WHY CAN'T WE GET IT RIGHT?

SECOND EDITION

SECOND EDITION

WHY CAN'T WE GET IT RIGHT?

Designing High-Quality Professional Development for Standards-Based Schools

Marsha Speck • Caroll Knipe

Foreword by Dennis Sparks

CORWIN PRESS
A Sage Publications Company
Thousand Oaks, California

For information:

Corwin Press
A Sage Publications Company
2455 Teller Road
Thousand Oaks, California 91320
www.corwinpress.com

Sage Publications Ltd.
1 Oliver's Yard
55 City Road
London EC1Y 1SP
United Kingdom

Sage Publications India Pvt. Ltd.
B-42, Panchsheel Enclave
Post Box 4109
New Delhi 110 017 India

Printed in the United States of America

Library of Congress Cataloging-in-Publication Data

Speck, Marsha.
Why can't we get it right?: Designing high-quality professional development for standards-based schools / by Marsha Speck and Caroll Knipe.—2nd ed.
    p. cm.
Includes bibliographical references and index.
ISBN 1-4129-0651-2 (cloth) — ISBN 1-4129-0652-0 (pbk.)
    1. Teachers—Inservice training. 2. Teachers—Training of.
I. Knipe, Caroll. II. Title.
LB1731.S683 2005
370'.71'55—dc22

                                    2004023095

This book is printed on acid-free paper.

05 06 07 08 09 10 9 8 7 6 5 4 3 2 1

Acquisitions Editor:	Rachel Livsey
Editorial Assistant:	Phyllis Cappello
Production Editor:	Laureen A. Shea
Copy Editor:	Cheryl Duksta
Typesetter:	C&M Digitals (P) Ltd.
Proofreader:	Christine K. Dahlin
Indexer:	Kay M. Dusheck
Graphic Designer:	Lisa Miller

Contents

Foreword

DEEP UNDERSTANDING,
EMPOWERING BELIEFS, INFORMED ACTION

In the second edition of *Why Can't We Get It Right? Designing High-Quality Professional Development for Standards-Based Schools*, Marsha Speck and Caroll Knipe provide a thorough overview of what is known about the nature of professional development that produces high levels of learning and performance for teachers and their students. They admirably achieve their goal of showing how well-designed professional development with a clear focus on improved student learning can make a difference in teaching and student success. Such professional development, they inform their readers, provides "both the challenge and support for educators to grow, change, and reflect on their practices."

Speck and Knipe tell us that high-quality professional development uses data in planning and evaluation, promotes reflection on current practice and the effectiveness of new approaches, and aligns strategies with school and district goals. It is grounded in high standards and systems of accountability, sustains effort over the months and years that mastery of complex skills requires, and applies leading-edge knowledge about teaching and learning. In addition, high-quality professional development deepens teachers' content knowledge and assessment expertise within that content, is embedded in the day-to-day tasks of teaching, draws on internal and external sources of expertise, engages teachers as leaders of staff development efforts as well as learners, extends into the classroom through modeling and coaching, and promotes collaborative interaction and inquiry among teachers.

Sometimes, though, it is possible for educational leaders who seek to improve professional learning to lose a sense of direction and feel overwhelmed by all the things they might be doing. As I perused *Why Can't We Get It Right?*, I found myself thinking about the 80/20 principle. In his book *The 80/20 Principle: The Secret to Success by Achieving More With Less*, Richard Koch says that this principle is based on the observation that "a minority of causes, inputs, or effort usually lead to a majority of the results, outputs, or rewards." The implications for professional development—or any other field of endeavor—is that some strategies or approaches are more powerful than others and that by focusing on them with laser-like intensity resources can be applied more effectively to produce intended results. The challenge, of course, is to know which of the many things we could be doing will turn out to be among the 20% of factors that produce 80% of the benefits.

Consequently, as I examined the recommendations offered by Speck and Knipe through the lens of my more than twenty-five years of experience in this field, I identified the elements that I believe are most powerful in creating improved student learning: Teachers use data and other forms of evidence to select student learning goals and to determine the effectiveness of their professional development in achieving those goals. Each day, teachers alone and together strengthen their lessons, deepen their understanding of what they teach, acquire new means to teach it, and create stronger bonds with their colleagues and students. They do so in cultures that are trusting, collaborative, and promote mutual accountability, cultures created by principals and teacher leaders.

Creating a system of professional learning and collaboration for all teachers is far more difficult, of course, than writing a few sentences, a foreword, or even a book about it. "Transforming schools and increasing student performance is not an easy process," Knipe and Speck acknowledge. "Nor is transforming professional learning for teachers and school leaders. That observation brings us back to the question posed in the title *Why Can't We Get It Right?*"

Those who read this book carefully and who seriously ponder the questions it poses will deepen their understanding of quality professional development. But understanding by itself is usually insufficient to "get it right." Consequently, I also encourage readers to use this book to examine and challenge their beliefs about professional learning (e.g., whether they believe that high-quality professional learning is truly essential in improving the quality of teaching in a school) and to commit themselves to significantly enhancing the quality of professional learning in their schools within a year through sustained, disciplined action. Understanding that is not aligned with empowering beliefs and supported by informed action will be of little value to the students who are now in our schools and who deserve high-quality teaching no matter in what classroom or school they find themselves.

Dennis Sparks
Executive Director, National Staff Development Council

Preface

One of the most powerful indicators of a successful school is teacher competence, described as teachers who know their content and strategies so well that they can open a virtual toolbox and take out information or processes they need so that all students can be successful. The idea that no child would be left behind was conceived not to diminish the high expectations of teachers but to be certain that all children have the opportunity to be successful and can count on support, encouragement, and expertise to give them an equal chance.

Since 1997, when Linda Darling-Hammond published her landmark book *The Right To Learn*, researchers, professors, school administrators, parents, and teachers have challenged each other to create the circumstances to cause each child to be successful. With the notion that each child has a right to learn was the underlying premise that each teacher has a right to the most current information, strategies, teaching conditions, and professional learning the schools could offer. Teachers took the premise of student success a step further. They became designers of their learning. They formed collaborative teams to study data, draw conclusions about failure and success, and practice new strategies evaluated for effectiveness. As teachers achieved mastery, they taught and coached others, investing more time in building their capacity as professionals in their classrooms and schools. We chronicled their processes and work in our first edition, *Why Can't We Get It Right? Professional Development in Our Schools.*

The second edition of *Why Can't We Get It Right? Designing High-Quality Professional Development for Standards-Based Schools* is intended to give teachers, teacher leaders, professors, supervisors, and administrators an edge in the race for personal efficacy and collective power focused on student achievement. Since our book was published in 2000, numerous practitioners have asked us for the following: a smaller text that would fit into notebooks, more tools to accomplish the work, less on history and more on action, key points to help review chapters, and open-ended scenarios as reflective tools. We welcomed their suggestions and made revisions. Each chapter is designed to begin with a brief scenario that serves as a discussion point to ground readers in the authenticity of the work.

Essential questions provoke deeper thought about each topic. To assure readers that professionals have evaluated the concepts over time, we included the research. Complete with graphics to illustrate the text, the body of each chapter provides information and challenges current practice. In some chapters, a blank frame is provided after the completed example so that readers can try out the ideas as they reflect on how to use the conceptual frameworks to improve their schools. Key points at the end of each chapter serve as reminders to busy professionals of the chapter content.

We hope that leaders will select the most meaningful and relevant chapters to digest, reflect on with colleagues, and incorporate into their collective actions for one purpose: to improve student achievement. Because the meaning of adventure includes spirit and excitement, we welcome our readers to the adventure of exploring *Why Can't We Get It Right? Designing High-Quality Professional Development for Standards-Based Schools.*

Acknowledgments

The role of professional development in helping schools, individuals, and districts continue to learn and evolve is both challenging and vital. We have been inspired and informed by those who have kept a clear focus on student achievement through their thoughts and actions in classrooms, schools, and districts. We wish to acknowledge their daily efforts to develop their skills, strategies, and attitudes essential to improving schools.

For expanding the role of professional development in learning and leading in the public schools, we thank the pioneers of our field, Roland Barth, Linda Darling-Hammond, Linda Lambert, Ann Lieberman, Lynne Miller, Judith Warren-Little, Dennis Sparks, and Stephanie Hirsh. Because of them we have been able to formulate, clarify, and reflect on our vision of professional development as a pathway to improved student achievement.

Thank you Rachel Livsey, our editor at Corwin Press, for your faith and encouragement for writing a second edition of our book on professional development with direct pathways to student achievement. Corwin Press has provided the means to share our work, and we are appreciative.

We are also appreciative of the personal and professional enrichment provided us by the following organizations: the Association of California School Administrators, the California School Leadership Academy, the California Staff Development Council, the National Staff Development Council, and the San Jose State University of California. These organizations have provided us with opportunities to make a difference in the lives of students.

We are indebted to and wish to thank our families for understanding the countless hours our work took and for encouraging us throughout the process. These wonderful individuals stood by us through it all and kept our work and life in perspective. Sincere thanks to Sue Webber for being a realist and seeing us through the early stages of critique and proofing, in addition to the entire endless process. Grateful appreciation is given to Marsha's sister, Linda McBain, for providing wonderful hospitality after a difficult day of writing. Special thanks go to Caroll's husband, Fritz, for his sense of humor and thoughtful insights and to son Randy Price, daughter Pam Winaker, son Gene Knipe, and daughter Heidi Knipe Lyons for sharing and listening.

Finally, we need to acknowledge our own unique and delightful collaborative work. Our thoughts, actions, and reflections on what matters most about professional development have been enriched, challenged, and supported by our work together. We approach our work with passion and commitment to improving schools to make a difference in teaching, learning, and student achievement.

The contributions of the following reviewers are gratefully acknowledged:

Joan Roberts
Retired School Administrator
Sedona, AZ

Dr. Marty Krovetz
Professor of Educational Leadership
San Jose State University
San Jose, CA

About the Authors

Marsha Speck, EdD, is a leader in school reform, educational leadership, and professional development issues. She is currently Professor of Educational Leadership at San Jose State University and Director of the Urban High School Leadership Program, an innovative project that brings together regional school district teacher leaders and administrators to rethink the American high school and how it works. She has diverse experience as a teacher, a high school principal, an assistant superintendent of instruction, a professor, and an author of three books and numerous articles and reports. She can be reached at mslvtennis@aol.com.

Caroll Knipe, MEd, recognized leader and educational planner, is committed to school change for student success. As veteran teacher, site administrator, leadership consultant, journal contributor, published author (*Why Can't We Get It Right? Professional Development in Our Schools*), university adjunct staff, academy director, speaker, coach, strategic positioner, and director of personnel, communications, and curriculum, Caroll has invested 40 years in public education. For fourteen years as executive director of the California School Leadership Academy in the Silicon Valley, Caroll facilitated premier leadership development programs recognized nationally and internationally. As president of the 15,000-member Association of California School Administrators (ACSA), she helped to set the state's educational direction. Her presentations include nationwide television seminars by Apple Computers; instructional television series, with roles as moderator and panelist; radio talk shows in Washington, DC, Los Angeles, and San Francisco; and facilitation at conferences for ACSA, the Association for Supervision and Curriculum Development, California and National Staff

Development Councils, and the California School Board Association. Recognized for outstanding leadership by state and national associations, she holds a bachelor's degree from Lock Haven State University in Pennsylvania and a master's degree from Western Washington State University. She can be reached at knilodge@garlic.com.

We dedicate this book to our families who have supported
our work and writing by encouraging us to pursue our passion
of improving education through quality professional development:

To Marsha's parents, James and Patricia
Gurney, who valued education and made sacrifices

To Caroll's husband, Fritz, an educator of excellence for forty years;
to our children Randy, Pam, Gene, and Heidi, who give meaning to our lives;
and to our exceptional grandchildren, Carly, Ryan, Matthew, Michael, Wesley, and
Taylor, our personal reasons for continuing the quest for high-quality public education

We also dedicate this book to principals and teachers who are
redesigning their schools to improve achievement for all students.
These professionals have dared to make a difference in teaching
and learning for themselves, their colleagues, and their students.

1

Essential Questions About High-Quality Professional Development

SCENARIO

Three teachers discussed their day as they walked to the parking lot after school. Their conversation turned to other topics.

Josie: *I just heard a report from the Education Trust in Washington, DC. I don't want to believe what Kati Haycock said. Did you know that out of every 100 Hispanic kindergarten children, only 61 will graduate from high school, and only 10 will get bachelor's degrees? She gave statistics for the other groups, but this one reached right into my heart.*

Kim: *I heard that. High schools really have a problem, don't they? I mean, obviously they aren't preparing kids for college.*

Jeff: *Do you really think it's their problem?*

Based on your experiences and learning, how would you and your colleagues respond?

ESSENTIAL QUESTION

To provide the best teaching and learning opportunities for the achievement of all students, what are the essential questions we must ask about professional development practices?

Pause for a moment to reflect on this essential question.

Prior reform efforts have not been buttressed by the ongoing professional development needed to prepare teachers to teach in the complex ways that learner-centered practice demands.

—Darling-Hammond (1997, p. xv)

INTRODUCTION

Comprehensive professional development for educators has generally been a neglected or shallow component of school reform efforts for the past twenty years. To increase student achievement and help all students meet the standards, educators must be well prepared. They must also engage in continuous learning to meet the demands of a changing and diverse student population in a rapidly evolving world. At the core of what schools and districts should be about is recognition of the need for continuous professional growth. No longer can school reform efforts tolerate shallow professional development that never really gets to the heart of providing in-depth experiences for new learning. If reform efforts are to take place, we cannot afford to let quality professional development get lost in the shuffle of shifting reform priorities and the countless time demands that affect the daily lives of teachers, school leaders, and district leaders. Just as a clear focus on student standards provides clarity of required achievement, so is a clear focus on professional development key to building the capacity of educators to help students achieve the standards and sustain their efforts over time. Research has shown that improving educators' (teachers' and leaders') knowledge and skills is a prerequisite to raising student performance.

The goal of this book is to deepen educators' collective understanding about how to create professional development opportunities and practices in a design that enables teachers to educate all students well. To sustain focused efforts, a well-designed professional development program will nourish the growth of educators and foster a learner-centered environment. If we are to dramatically improve schools and schooling, we must insist on professional development designs and practices that make a difference in teacher learning and student success. The professional learning, therefore, will permeate the system, resulting in higher academic results for students. When district offices, parents, communities, county and state departments of education, educators' associations, and state and federal legislators recognize and support these designs and practices, and when all of these groups align their goals with student achievement, the key elements will be in place for responding to the question in the title *Why Can't We Get It Right?*

In framing the book, we challenge readers with essential questions regarding professional development to focus the discussion for each chapter and to cause readers to reflect on their current professional development practices.

Professional development opportunities and practices must provide both the challenge and the support for educators to grow, change, and reflect on their practices. Creating such opportunities requires commitment, understanding, planning, resources, time, and evaluation. This book provides the reader with knowledge, insights, tools, and designs to assist in creating new professional development opportunities that serve the learner-centered school and improve student achievement.

Educational leaders and teachers must design programs to support professional growth along a continuum of each educator's experience to be learner centered and learning centered. The failure by most schools and districts to recognize the importance and need for continuous, aligned, needs-based professional development condemns school reform efforts to ultimate failure. Virtually every effort to improve education since the publication of *A Nation at Risk* (National Commission on Excellence in Education, 1983) has centered on overcoming deficits in student knowledge or dealing with reshaping the structure and organization of schooling. School reform efforts—ranging from increased course content and rigor to establishing charter schools, from testing schools for accountability to lowering class size, and from changing schedules to creating schools within schools—all have largely left the classroom untouched (Sparks & Hirsh, 1999). Thus, teachers, despite reformers' efforts, generally continue to teach as they have in the past. No wonder we have seen little or no increase in student results. Research and proven practice demonstrate that expanding teacher knowledge and improving teaching skills are essential to raising student achievement (Darling-Hammond, 1997). In the redefinition of teacher and student needs, we have created a new meaning of professional development.

WHAT IS HIGH-QUALITY PROFESSIONAL DEVELOPMENT?

High-quality professional development is a sustained collaborative learning process that systematically nourishes the growth of educators (individuals and teams) through adult learner-centered, job-embedded processes. It focuses on educators' attaining the skills, abilities, and deep understandings needed to improve student achievement.

It is the authors' premise that in schools the focus of professional development must be to improve student learning. As fostered in a learner-centered environment, professional development is embedded in the daily work of educators; offers choices and levels of learning; builds on collaborative, shared knowledge; employs effective teaching and assessment strategies; expands teacher knowledge of learning and development; and informs teachers' daily work. It is sustained and intensive, with opportunities for practice, collaborative application through problem solving and action research, mastery, coaching, and leadership. Professional development includes an evaluation of progress as it builds teacher and leadership capacity and as it affects student learning.

The lack of professional development, as well as its misuse by educators, explains the chronic failure of school reform. New professional development models exist that will help propel school reform efforts when used systematically over time. The knowledge, skills, attitudes, behaviors, and practices of teaching are only minimally challenged by current practice. In addition, districts do not provide consistent support and leadership for improving teaching practice. If this is the dilemma, what essential questions should educators ask that would cause them to rethink their current professional development practices?

Essential Questions for High-Quality Professional Development

Essential questions challenge educators' thoughts about professional development practices and help us transform schools into vibrant learning centers for both students and educators (Table 1.1). The questions help shift the focus from what is to what could be. They engage educators in a reflective process that generates new ideas and designs. They help teachers and administrators in schools continue their growth and challenge their current practices in professional development. Through the examination of professional development practices, educators will better understand what it takes to bring about change and reforms in education that can be sustained to support all students and their success. We challenge the reader to think deeply and reflect on the essential questions for high-quality professional development (Table 1.1), which provide a focus for each chapter in this book.

Examining the big picture (Figure 1.1, see p. 6) provides the reader with a visual of the interactions of the focus areas and the corresponding essential questions. The dynamics of professional development designs and tools interconnect to help drive the outcome of student achievement using the improvement process. As you view the dynamics, you can see that the processes and conditions for high-quality professional development are

Table 1.1   Essential Questions for High-Quality Professional Development

- To provide the best teaching and learning opportunities for the achievement of all students, what are the essential questions we must ask about professional development practices?

- How will schools and districts design professional development opportunities and policies that create, shape, and sustain the culture of a learning community focused on student achievement? (Chapter 2)

- What conditions and processes using cycles of improvement (inquiry) will be used to address high-quality professional development focused on student achievement while addressing teacher, team, and school concerns? (Chapter 3)

- What professional development designs and tools will be used to focus a learning community on student achievement? (Chapter 4)

- How will schools and districts evaluate their professional development programs based on student achievement and continuous improvement? (Chapter 5)

- What expertise, knowledge, and tools do we need to rethink professional learning in the schools? (Chapter 6)

interwoven and not linear. Each of the parts is working simultaneously in the learning community to create a force for sustainable change to increase student achievement. Visualize the dynamics in motion within your own school. Are there missing pieces? Why?

We hope that by reading each chapter, your own experience, knowledge, and subsequent reflections will add to your understanding of how to provide high-quality professional development, leading to increased student achievement.

THE CHANGE PROCESS FOR SUSTAINING EDUCATIONAL IMPROVEMENT

Educators need to explore the change process for sustaining educational improvement, recognizing the simplicity of the concept and the complexity of implementation. The visual representation of the change process (Figure 1.2, see p. 7) provides a conceptual framework of the interactive components supported by research and proven practice. Because of the interactive qualities of the parts, no one element is more important than the others, and, conversely, no one element can be omitted if the design is to be successful. It is of critical importance that the focus is on improving

Figure 1.1 Big Picture: Focus of and Essential Questions for Professional Development

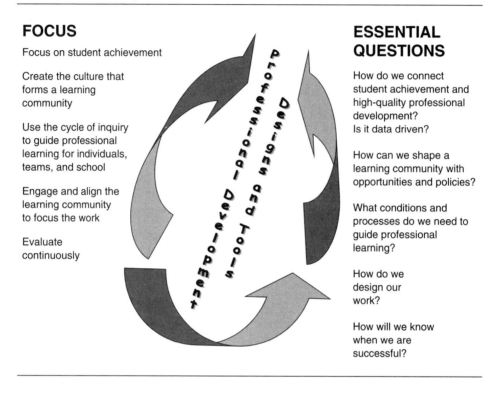

FOCUS

Focus on student achievement

Create the culture that forms a learning community

Use the cycle of inquiry to guide professional learning for individuals, teams, and school

Engage and align the learning community to focus the work

Evaluate continuously

ESSENTIAL QUESTIONS

How do we connect student achievement and high-quality professional development?
Is it data driven?

How can we shape a learning community with opportunities and policies?

What conditions and processes do we need to guide professional learning?

How do we design our work?

How will we know when we are successful?

student learning and achievement. This is a change from past practice. Prior to the emphasis on standards, educators considered professional development to be whatever someone in the system thought interesting or useful. Without the focus on improving student learning, educators often could not connect what happened in one year with the next. In fact, using "the pendulum swings" as an excuse for waiting for the next change—not doing any serious thinking about the current thrust because it would be gone next year—is a direct consequence of unfocused professional development practices. Anticipating four to seven years for the change process to become culturally significant allows educators to continuously analyze needs using a data-driven process centered on student achievement. Designing the work within a learning community provides a foundation for improvement using ongoing monitoring systems and job-embedded professional development practices.

Addressing the essentials illustrated in Figure 1.2 (focuses on improved student achievement with needs assessment, creates a school culture, provides professional development, and evaluates goals) in a systematic way through relevant content and interactive processes provides coherence and sustainability to ongoing professional development plans

Figure 1.2 Essentials for High-Quality Professional Development Sustained Educational Change Model

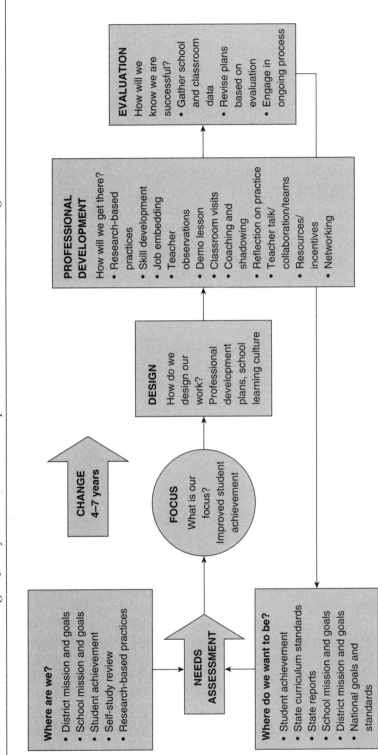

Where are we?
- District mission and goals
- School mission and goals
- Student achievement
- Self-study review
- Research-based practices

NEEDS ASSESSMENT

Where do we want to be?
- Student achievement
- State curriculum standards
- State reports
- School mission and goals
- District mission and goals
- National goals and standards

CHANGE 4–7 years

FOCUS
What is our focus?
Improved student achievement

DESIGN
How do we design our work?
Professional development plans, school learning culture

PROFESSIONAL DEVELOPMENT
How will we get there?
- Research-based practices
- Skill development
- Job embedding
- Teacher observations
- Demo lesson
- Classroom visits
- Coaching and shadowing
- Reflection on practice
- Teacher talk/collaboration/teams
- Resources/incentives
- Networking

EVALUATION
How will we know we are successful?
- Gather school and classroom data
- Revise plans based on evaluation
- Engage in ongoing process

and actions. If one views a school district's design of professional development over a period of years, one can often see that these key essentials have been neglected, especially the components of keeping a clear focus on improving student achievement and of evaluating procedures to meet the goals. These essentials of the high-quality professional development for sustaining educational change model emphasize the need for a long-term (four- to seven-year period), ongoing commitment to practices. We can no longer afford to jump from one professional development activity to the next, year after year, but must be strategic about seeing professional development embedded in our school planning and culture, data analysis and decision making, and resource support of teachers, principals, and staff professionals learning to improve practice.

Elements of High-Quality Professional Development

If educators have a clear image of what high-quality professional development entails, such an image will help them evaluate and design their own professional development opportunities. The elements in Figure 1.3 are designed as critical elements to help the reader understand the key components necessary for developing professional development plans that will bring about change in current educational practice. Although Figure 1.3 depicts a cyclic process of inquiry, the reader should keep in mind that all parts are essential for the total design to be effective. These elements provide a framework for understanding the essential parts of designing quality professional development. Each element is briefly discussed as to its importance and its relationship to high-quality professional development based on research and proven practice.

Focuses on Improving Student Learning

High-quality professional development must focus on conditions for improving student learning and achievement. Student success is the ultimate aim and outcome of well-planned professional development (Guskey, 2000; Joyce & Showers, 1995). The needs of all students, especially in our diverse society, must inform all aspects of a professional development design. We cannot afford to lose sight of this goal in the process of designing a professional development program. Professional development focused on improved student learning will prevent a disconnect from occurring between the purpose of the professional development and the process. Once this overarching goal has been established, the content, processes, materials, and evaluations of professional development efforts can be measured according to whether they support this goal. Components that fail to improve student learning can be dropped, modified, or redesigned (Steiner, as cited in Hassel, 1999).

Figure 1.3   Elements of High-Quality Professional Development (Includes Both Content and Process)

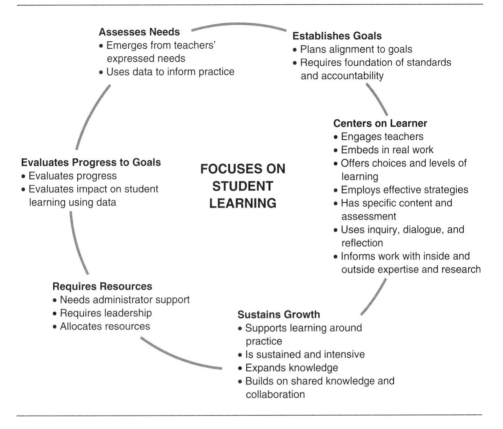

Districts and schools must focus all professional development plans on improving student learning and achievement. Teachers, schools, and districts must hold a clear, sustained, systemic focus on specific areas for improving student learning (i.e., literacy) over several (three to five or more) years for lasting change to occur and improvement to be shown (Schmoker, 1996). If learning and professional growth are supported and reinforced, then there cannot be a year-by-year change of focus. Little (1993b) asserts that highly effective schools are those that are able to weather the conflicting policy mandates and practices to which they are subjected and maintain a clear path with well-established goals.

Recently, there have been signs that districts and schools are truly beginning to understand that there is a need for focus and coherence in their professional development plans if student learning is to improve. Research and experience confirm that the difference for students between a well-prepared teacher and a poorly prepared teacher can be a full level of achievement in a single year (Haycock, 1999). Quality professional development can produce immediate gains in teacher quality, which affects student achievement (Cohen & Hill, 1998). Where does your school or district stand in understanding the true importance of sustaining a focus on improving student learning, both in planning and action taken, through professional development opportunities?

Assesses Needs and Establishes Goals

Emerges From Teachers' Expressed Needs. Professional development can emerge from teachers' expressed, and sometimes urgent, need to know. When leaders respond to teachers' expressed professional development needs, which emerge from teachers' daily work with students, the design for professional growth becomes meaningful and immediate (Lieberman & Miller, 1999). Leaders, especially principals, must have the ability to listen to teachers and understand their emerging needs as changes take place and as professional development is adapted to the learning environment. It is difficult for teachers to focus on district-imposed professional development when their immediate concerns are not being addressed. Meeting teacher-felt needs is the foundation for building future professional development plans. A direct connection must be established between the teachers' felt needs and the students' achievement levels and needs; this connection can be made by examining student work and allowing teachers to define their areas of needed professional growth (Schmoker, 1996). To do this, school leaders must work collaboratively with teachers to provide multiple experiences to help teachers—as well as themselves—identify needs in both content knowledge and instructional skills to better meet individual student needs (Darling-Hammond & Ball, 1998).

Uses Data to Inform Practice and Make Decisions. Because accountability for student learning is the focus, designers of professional development should use disaggregated data on student achievement and needs as well as information about teachers' skills and abilities to inform the design. If data analysis does not occur, then professional development plans may be based on misinformation, and training may be initiated that is neither necessary nor useful. Processes must be in place to inform teachers about student achievement data, causing them to analyze the data and look for areas of strength and needed improvement. These assessment processes will show the gaps in student learning and in teacher competence. Then, decisions about which professional development needs to take place are based on a thorough analysis that includes student work and achievement levels and the alignment with standards. Too often, professional plans are drafted without reviewing data, and prescriptive activities are simply mandated for teachers. The latest fads and programs cannot be sought to fix the problems. Meaningful analysis that requires teachers and leaders to see patterns and trends provides for understanding and informed decision making about professional development needs and plans.

Aligns Plans Systematically With School and District Change Efforts and Goals.
If real change and progress is to be accomplished, professional development plans must be aligned systematically with school- and districtwide
goals and change efforts. Aligning school and district professional development opportunities sends a clear message about the direction of the district and supports a better use of district resources (Joyce & Showers, 1995).
Alignment provides the coherence necessary for long-term commitment
to school and district goals and results. How often have school- and districtwide plans lacked focus, jumping from one professional development
activity to the next with no aligned, systemic, long-term plan? Aligned
school- and districtwide systems and structures need to be in place for
effective, career-long professional development (Darling-Hammond &
McLaughlin, 1995). Thus, linking professional development to the educational goals of the school and district is essential for achieving significant
change (Steiner, as cited in Hassel, 1999).

Bases Professional Development on a Foundation of Standards and Accountability.
Professional development plans must be based on a foundation of standards and accountability. Standards provide the starting point for developing plans, a focus, and outcomes for professional development. If
educators are committed to students' meeting the standards, then they
must have a clear understanding of the content and an ability to teach to
the standards. Professional development plans and opportunities must be
tied to standards and appropriate assessments; otherwise, the curriculum
has no anchor. Teachers must also see a clear link between professional
development, student learning, standards, and accountability (Sparks &
Hirsh, 1997).

Accountability for the outcomes of professional development is vital
in relation to increased student achievement and school improvement. A
professional development plan or activity that demonstrates its purpose
through specific outcomes tied to school or district goals shows its worth
in a critical way. Educators can no longer afford simply to have a professional development activity without related accountability. If the professional development is valuable, then it should be demonstrated through
the achievement of clear outcomes. Specific expectations are important for
professional development (Guskey, 2000). Participants must know what
has been accomplished and what needs to be done. Schools or districts
investing in professional development should require results; otherwise,
why invest?

Centers on the Learner

Engages Teachers in Planning, Implementing, Reviewing, and Revising. Often
professional development is designed by outside experts or district office
staff and then imposed on teachers as a quick fix to raise failing student

achievement. Unless teachers are engaged in planning, implementing, reviewing, evaluating, and revising professional development plans with their school and district on a regular basis, they will probably not commit to the outcomes (Darling-Hammond & McLaughlin, 1995). Because teachers are the recipients of professional development, they should have significant ownership and a deeper understanding of the plans (Lieberman, 1995). The development of ownership and commitment to improved practice are important to ensure positive participation by faculty in professional development. Because teachers are affected by change, they must have input into the changes, or there is no meaning in their involvement. Engaged teachers can plan, give feedback, review, and revise professional development based on their working knowledge, understanding of student learning needs, and commitment to the plan. Too often, school leaders undermine the legitimacy and effectiveness of professional development by failing to include participants in planning and delivery (Corcoran, 1995).

Offers Choices and Levels of Learning. A variety of choices and levels of learning in professional development provides participants with options based on their own learning needs. Educators' recognition that one-size-fits-all professional development will not meet the needs of all participants is an important concept in designing professional development for the wide range of abilities found within a school or district (Sparks & Hirsh, 1997). Understanding the current developmental level of the participants allows a planner to challenge individuals to improve based on their current abilities within a focused area. Honoring the developmental levels and experiences of teachers through appropriate means is critical to the professional development design. Once teachers and administrators establish the specific needs for learning, then a variety of choices and strategies for learning can be offered to individuals to improve their professional competence. These multiple entry points, based on individual teacher needs and skill levels, will focus professional development in specific areas.

Teachers are tired of professional development that is imposed on them from the top. Such professional development plans are presented as being good for all, rather than being balanced by recognition of individual strengths and areas of personal improvement. Effective professional development has multiple opportunities, is diverse, and provides for an ongoing process as it actively engages the educator in learning. Districts and schools must recognize this complexity and the differentiated need to implement successful professional development that meets teachers' needs and improves student performance. Teachers feel a greater sense of commitment to change and more interest in participating in professional development when attention is paid to their assessed needs (Duke et al., as cited in Collins, 1998). This important analysis and understanding of individual as well as schoolwide needs make it possible to plan professional development efforts that recognize the teachers' felt needs, content knowledge level, and skill gaps (Guskey, 1999).

Embeds in Real Work of the Teachers. Embedding professional development in the real work of teachers provides for clear connections to their work with students and to the improvement of student achievement. This relevancy and context of professional development allow teachers to inquire, reflect, analyze, and act on their current practice, especially as they examine student work and learning and their ability to provide increased learning for their students. Professional development is not an isolated event that takes place outside the school but rather an integrated part of the daily work of teachers. The experiences of learning together emerge from real work together (Lieberman & Miller, 1999). Such professional development ignites commitment and continual growth based on the unique circumstances of the teacher and the school. It becomes an integral part of a teacher's professional life as the school develops the ecology of a learning community.

However, Guskey (1999) cautions that these professional development needs must be more deeply analyzed to make sure that schoolwide (not just individual) needs are accurately identified. This critical analysis requires planning and a team effort by teachers and staff to close common student learning and teacher skill gaps (Guskey, 1999). When professional development is seen as a daily integrated part of a teacher's work life, there is a recognition within the school culture that learning needs, adjustments, the search for new ideas and skills, and reflection on current teaching practices are embedded in the daily life of the teacher and school.

Employs Effective Teaching and Learning Strategies. Understanding the learning styles of participants and providing multiple strategies for learning allow individual learning needs to be met through the professional development process. Educators recognize that not all individuals learn in the same way at the same time. Using a variety of effective learning strategies (e.g., media, the Internet, dramatic presentations, dialogue, or other collaborative processes) enhances the participants' abilities to process, understand, and learn new information and skills. This diversification gives participants several pathways to knowing and understanding, which moves well beyond the knowledge level of learning. A variety of techniques can reinforce learning in a number of ways, allowing individuals to process and internalize new information in different contexts with various learning modalities. For continuous professional growth to occur, professional development plans must include these multiple strategies to recognize learners' developmental, as well as career-level, needs and experiences (Wood & Thompson, 1993).

Has Content Specific to Teaching and Assessment of Subject Matter. Professional development cannot ignore the integration of specific subject matter content along with teaching and assessment development for teachers. Professional growth opportunities that specifically address how the new information and strategies affect teaching and assessment in particular subject matter areas get to the heart of how the new learning will be implemented. Vague references to applications of new teaching and assessment techniques to content with no examples of what works in the classroom will not advance professional growth. Teachers need rich examples, modeling, practice, and coaching embedded in subject areas. New literacy strategies, such as the use of organizers to focus learning, should be modeled in professional development seminars, practiced in the context of the classroom, and shared with colleagues for feedback and refinement. The more the strategies use actual subject matter content, the greater the learning for participants. Including assessment strategies (e.g., running records and personal word lists in reading professional development seminars) provides teachers with specific, integrated strategies to evaluate student progress. Application to the content area gives clear messages about the relationships between content and assessment and how to apply strategies in the classroom (Darling-Hammond, Ancess, & Falk, 1995).

Uses Inquiry, Dialogue, and Reflection to Inform Practice. Cycles of inquiry, dialogue, and reflection provide the means for thoughtful discussion of important learning issues in a school or district. Engaging in a cycle of inquiry requires educators to examine their current practices and outcomes, engage in dialogues about these practices, conduct inquiry into what research and best practices say, and reflect on what was learned from the study before taking corrective action. Informing practice using these inquiry processes will make a difference for student learning. It is this cycle of inquiry that challenges educational practices and encourages teachers to develop professionally (Darling-Hammond, 1997; Sagor, 1992; Schmoker, 1996).

Informs Work With Inside and Outside Expertise and Research. Balancing the use of inside and outside expertise and research to inform professional practice in schools and districts is critical (Lieberman & Miller, 1999). The needed and valuable expertise of practitioners within the school, combined with the new knowledge and strategies of outside expertise and research, provides a healthy balance in a system. Informing professional practices by using valued, inside teacher expertise helps provide experiences that sustain the ongoing aspects of professional development in a school. An outside expert can provide new knowledge and even coaching (Joyce & Showers, 1995, 1996, 2002). Teachers then need to practice, reflect on, and refine the strategies over time in their classrooms. Research and outside expertise bring new knowledge and practices to the school setting. This outside expertise and information must be understood and adapted by practitioners to the context of their students and schools. Little change will occur unless current practices are examined and challenged by teachers as new knowledge and strategies are internalized. Using inside expertise (i.e., peer coaches, expert coaches for novices, trainer of trainer models) to help implement, refine, or review practice helps teachers to recognize their own levels of expertise and to feel the power of sharing with colleagues on an ongoing basis. Professional practice is balanced and reinforced by the professional development process of combining inside and outside expertise and research (Lieberman & Miller, 1999).

Sustains Growth

Supports Learning Around Practice With Modeling, Coaching, and Problem Solving. New learning must be supported by modeling, coaching, and problem-solving components for the new learning to be practiced, reflected on, and integrated into regular use by the learner. Professional development that does not model or include the critical element of ongoing modeling and coaching lacks the continuous support needed for individuals to change practice (Joyce & Showers, 1995, 1996, 2002). If teachers are condemned to onetime or fragmented workshops with little or no modeling, follow-up, coaching, analysis of problems, and adjustment in practice, there will be little change. Just as with sports or music, modeling, practice, coaching, and analysis of performance help hone the skills of the individual. Why should learning new teaching concepts and strategies be different? These crucial elements of modeling, practicing, coaching, and problem solving will end the isolation of teachers and broaden the school into a community of learners in support of teaching and learning (Barth, 1990; Lieberman & Miller, 1999; Little, 1993a; Sparks & Hirsh, 1997). This concept of supporting the "learning organization" (Senge, 1990) within the normal working of a school day gives teachers and administrators the time for the inquiry, reflection, and mentoring necessary for long-term change in practice.

Is Sustained and Intensive With Opportunities for Mastery and Leadership. If individual educators are to continue their personal growth, they must have multiple opportunities for participation with an in-depth approach that is intensive and sustained over a period of time (Darling-Hammond, 1997). Educators need quality time to master new strategies and new learning by practicing them in their classrooms, reflecting on these practices, and refining their learning. Mastery comes only with study, practice, coaching, feedback, and refinement in a sustained effort. As teachers develop mastery, they can provide leadership in helping others understand the concepts and develop their skills. Encouraging leadership by teachers recognizes their expertise, which can be used to help others, and builds the capacity of the school and district (Lambert, 1998).

Expands on Knowledge of Learning and Development. Continually expanding on teachers' current knowledge about learning and development provides the foundation of lifelong learning for educators. It validates the learning community concept within a school and district. Understanding the developing new research on learning and how it applies to what happens in the classroom helps inform and change practices, leading to increased student achievement. As educators, we can ill afford to retain practices that have not proven to be successful or to avoid the new knowledge being generated around learning and the developmental levels of children (Darling-Hammond & McLaughlin, 1995; Gardner, 1999; Lieberman, 1995).

Builds on Shared Knowledge of Teachers and Is Collaborative. Professional development must build on the shared knowledge of participants in a collaborative setting. As educators develop plans for professional improvement, they must understand the breadth of knowledge a faculty possesses and plan how to share that knowledge in a collaborative way. When the professional knowledge of teachers is untapped during professional development activities, facilitators create a hostile climate. If outside experts tell, rather than engage, teachers, the opportunity for a collaborative and collective sharing and expanding of baseline knowledge is lost. When leaders recognize the broad knowledge of teachers and commit to constructing collaborative processes to enable teachers to share that knowledge, they create a culture that nurtures continuous improvement and learning (i.e., action research, cycles of inquiry, trainer of trainer and peer coaching models; Joyce & Showers, 1995, 1996; Sagor, 1992; Sparks & Hirsh, 1997).

Requires Resources

Requires Administrative Support and Leadership and Allocates Resources. Administrative support is a key element in successful professional development planning and implementation. When administrators understand the importance of the professional development plan and how it affects student learning, their support is more easily garnered. Principals can provide support and recognition of the importance of the work through their leadership actions and allocated resources. When administrators support teachers in their professional development work with needed resources, including structured time, they send an important signal that professional development is to be taken seriously (Guskey, 2000; Schmoker, 1996). The leadership of administrators and teachers helps to establish a priority for professional development planning and implementation. Principals and other leaders need to be present and involved in professional development activities to learn, understand, and support the new learnings (Fullan, 1993). Through discourse and engagement in learning, teachers and administrators model a community of learners. Professional development without leadership and direction lacks the necessary commitment on the part of teachers and administrators to carry it out (Little, 1993a). Educators can easily become confused by the mixed message that is sent when leaders do not provide support and resources for professional development but still voice an expectation that teachers should learn and implement new strategies to raise student achievement.

Evaluates Progress to Goals

Evaluates Progress and Impact on Student Learning Using Data. Evaluating progress toward the goals of professional development and the impact on student learning is the accountability measure that gives credibility to the importance of continuous professional development. Unless evaluation of progress to date occurs, leaders have no evidence that the professional development is working. A systematic plan to collect data, analyze it, and make changes based on the significance of the data should inform professional development planners (Guskey, 2000). The evaluation process must go deeper than whether participants liked or disliked the activity. It must analyze whether teachers improved their practice and whether the changed practice affected student learning. What difference did the training make in the classroom? Looking long term at student data and the effect of specific professional development provides important feedback on the investment of a school or district in professional development. This continuous cycle of inquiry into practice causes educators to question current practices based on data and to seek new methods of improving their abilities to increase student achievement (Darling-Hammond, 1997; Sagor, 1992). A clear evaluation process requires both focused efforts and accountability for progress toward intended outcomes (Guskey, 2000).

SURVEY OF ELEMENTS OF HIGH-QUALITY PROFESSIONAL DEVELOPMENT

If schools or districts were to look at research-based elements of successful professional development as a set of questions regarding professional development opportunities, how would they respond? The Survey of Elements of High-Quality Professional Development (Table 1.2) is intended as a tool for analyzing current professional development practices within a school or district. In reality, these elements overlap, repeat, and often occur simultaneously. This assessment tool is intended to lead to reflection about professional development opportunities, not to overwhelm the reader. It is a tool by which key leverage points can be identified to improve professional development planning and implementation. By identifying these leverage points (specific elements) for professional development, schools and districts can clarify their goals, strategies, and

(Text continues on p. 20)

Table 1.2   Survey of Elements of High-Quality Professional Development

---

Directions: For each question, circle the number that best represents the answer as it relates to the current professional development program in your school or district based on the following scale: 1 = *never*, 2 = *seldom*, 3 = *usually*, 4 = *always*

1	**2**	**3**	**4**
Never	*Seldom*	*Usually*	*Always*

1. Is there a focus on improving student learning?

1	2	3	4

2. Does it emerge from teachers' expressed and sometimes urgent need to know?

1	2	3	4

3. Does it use data to inform practice and make decisions about teaching and learning?

1	2	3	4

4. Are the plans aligned systematically with school and district change efforts and goals?

1	2	3	4

5. Is it based on a foundation of standards and accountability?

1	2	3	4

6. Are teachers engaged in planning, implementing, reviewing, evaluating, and revising professional development plans?

1	2	3	4

7. Are individuals offered choices and levels of learning?

1	2	3	4

8. Is the professional development embedded in the real work of the teacher?

1	2	3	4

9. Does the professional development employ effective teaching and learning strategies?

1	2	3	4

10. Does it integrate content specific to teaching and assessment of subject matter?

                    1   2   3   4

11. Does it involve inquiry, dialogue, and reflection?

                    1   2   3   4

12. Does it inform work by using inside and outside expertise and research?

                    1   2   3   4

13. Does it support learning with modeling, coaching, and problem solving around practice?

                    1   2   3   4

14. Is it sustained and intensive with opportunities for mastery and leadership?

                    1   2   3   4

15. Does it expand on knowledge of learning and development?

                    1   2   3   4

16. Does it build on shared knowledge of teachers and provide for collaborative interaction?

                    1   2   3   4

17. Are there administrative support, internal leadership, and available resources?

                    1   2   3   4

18. Does it evaluate progress and measure impact on student learning?

                    1   2   3   4

Total score: _____ divided by 18 = _____

How does this score inform your professional development design and practices?

resources as they focus on student success. The survey provides a baseline assessment of a school or district's high-quality professional development practices, which can be used to evaluate the progress toward improving professional development practices and plans.

CONCLUSION

Transforming schools and increasing student performance is not an easy process. Educators in schools and districts that have a systematic approach to continuous professional development provide a pathway for improving student learning and achievement. Delineating what it means to develop, implement, evaluate, and revise professional development plans has been the intent of the discussion of the elements of successful professional development and the essential questions. Analyzing where your school and district stand in relation to quality professional development and your capacity to increase student learning is an important step to take. Transformation of schools will not happen overnight but must be nurtured over a period of time, with professional development that supports and facilitates the transformational process as teachers and leaders learn, practice, reflect, and grow together.

At the end of each chapter we have provided a space for reflection on the key points. Take a moment now and review the key points for Chapter 1. This chapter introduces the models used throughout this book.

Stop and reflect on these key points and their meaning for student achievement in your school.

KEY POINTS

- High-quality professional development is the critical leverage point for improving student learning and achievement.
- Essential questions for high-quality professional development drive the focus and work to achieve improved student learning. Each of these questions frames the focus for each chapter: focus on improving student achievement, plans and policies for learning culture, conditions and processes for the cycle of improvement, designs and tools, evaluation methods, and future trends.
- High-quality professional development is a sustained collaborative learning process that systematically nourishes the growth of

educators (individuals and teams) through adult learner-centered, job-embedded processes. It focuses on educators' attaining the skills, abilities, and deep understandings needed to improve student achievement.

- High-quality professional development has critical elements that must be addressed if professional educators are to grow and schools are to improve: assessing needs, establishing goals, centering on the learner, sustaining growth, requiring resources, and evaluating progress to goals.
- Key tables, figures, and a survey tool will assist in defining and assessing current and future school and district professional development plans and processes.

Note

The recommended readings and Web sites in Resources A and B will help educators design professional development processes and plans.

2

Creating the Culture for a Learning Community

SCENARIO

Two teachers, Gwen and Rosita, walked to their cars after the first day of school.

"I'm glad I could come to Redwood Hills after doing my student teaching here last year, but I'm worried. I'm going to have my hands full with this class," Gwen confided.

"Oh really? That's too bad," said Rosita.

"Do you think I should ask the third-grade teacher for some ideas? She had most of these kids last year!"

"That might give you some insights. Problem is," Rosita sighed, "teachers are so busy."

"So where do I go if I need help?"

Based on your learning and experience, what support systems, including professional development opportunities, can you identify for a new teacher in your school or district? Rate your responses on a scale of 1 to 5, with 5 being the most supportive of new teachers.

ESSENTIAL QUESTION

How will schools and districts design professional development opportunities and policies that create, shape, and sustain the culture of a learning community focused on student achievement?

Pause for a moment to reflect on this essential question.

THE ESSENCE OF A LEARNING COMMUNITY

When the culture of an organization is collaborative, each teacher has a built-in network of support. The role of a leader is not only to select the right people to be part of the organization but also to create an environment where they can succeed. In a learning community, the leader encourages all educators to develop a mind-set of collaboration, shared inquiry, and teamwork and then formalizes the structures necessary to support them. Continuous learning characterizes the learning community. New teachers and teachers new to a system are particularly at risk without a network of support. When the system provides what they need through, for example, coaching, mentoring, buddy systems, university partnerships, collaborative teams, or other on-site programs, the investment a district makes in the new teacher has potential for long-term rewards. It's very expensive to continuously hire teachers who then leave the school or district. Richard M. Ingersol and Thomas Smith (2003), in "The Wrong Solution to the Teacher Shortage," after studying the phenomenon for the past decade, stated, "The data suggest that after just five years, between 40 and 50 percent of all beginning teachers have left the profession" (p. 32). They claim that recruiting isn't the only response to the teacher shortage problem; retention of teachers also needs attention.

Is there progress in finding solutions or should the educational community throw up its collective hands in dismay and accept what is? Results from California's Beginning Teacher Support and Assessment (BTSA) study showed that a supportive program that included a powerful professional development component increased retention a remarkable 93% for first- and second-year teachers in the 1999–2000 school year. Teachers need support to be effective, and support offered in the beginning years for new teachers or those new to the system is critical.

The main challenge is to form a learning community to support improvement in teaching and learning. Linda Lambert, Deborah Walker, and their colleagues (1995) point to the new "enlightenment" with the advent of the learning community in the 1980s, which advanced some challenging assumptions, such as achievement is increased when the culture of the school supports learning for both students and adults. Lambert et al. supported the development of new norms that foster collaboration and shared inquiry. They also cited the initiation of the concept of a learning community as the first time researchers and educators placed a high value on teacher growth, linking teacher and student learning. "Collaborative teaching methods that promote learning for all students are applied to the organizational processes that characterize the school, so that the school becomes a learning organization (a continually renewing place to live and work)" (Lambert et al., 1995, p. 15). When a school lives in a culture of learning and working together, not only do educators rely more on each other's strengths, but also they are less reluctant to identify missing expertise. Do not accept that collaborative interaction is indicative of a lack of knowledge. In fact, collaboration is evidence of both faculty strength and a healthy school climate.

Sharon D. Kruse (1999) discusses being a new teacher in the only portable classroom at an elementary school in a Seattle suburb, half a football field away from the rest of the building: "What I gained in autonomy, independence, and opportunity for personal growth, I paid for in a loss of cooperative relationships, collegial support, and collaborative interaction" (p. 14). The second part of her article describes her new learning after she moved from the portable to the main building: "In the 'real' school building teachers may be closer to the bathrooms, but many are no less isolated, alone, and unsupported than I'd been in my portable" (p. 14). The realization was sobering for a new teacher who could project a professional career with no hope of receiving any future collegial support.

If we endorse the premises that many educators are isolated, that more is expected of them, and that they expect more from their careers than ever before, what can they do?

One important step is to formalize professional development policies that include collaborative interaction as a part of any new learning. In addition, successful schools include interactive time for teachers and administrators so that these educators have opportunities to be with other professionals. In a university class of thirty-five teachers, we asked participants to think of a team that they were members of at their site. Two students reported that they were not members of any team. Puzzled, we asked if they were at least part of grade-level or content teams. Again, the answer was negative. Even today, with the widely published research on collaborative inquiry in quality organizations, we still found principals who didn't acknowledge the power of teacher collaboration to improve student learning by formalizing a team structure and using collaborative time.

Educators are seeking a more expansive definition of professional success. The old strategies for teaching and learning aren't sufficient. More students should be graduating from high school with the skills and knowledge to succeed in their chosen university or career fields. How will teachers connect successfully with all students and create value in the system for them? These are huge demands on educators of today. Why then should teachers and administrators withhold professional expertise from each other? It makes no sense. They should be interacting and collaborating locally and nationally to explore how it is possible for them to serve all students in their schools.

Who has the time to make all of this happen? When the expectations, resources, scheduled opportunities, rewards, and recognition for collaborative action are built into school and district cultures, time to make it happen is woven into the fabric of the school community.

Boards of education and school administrators may push so hard to implement standards and raise test scores that they forget to put equal pressure on the system for high-quality professional learning, a collaborative environment, and time to make it happen. They are asking teachers to run a race by increasing the stride, yet when the stride is too long, the heel hits the ground at a bracing angle and acts as a brake to the long-distance runner. When educators strive to teach all standards to all students without professional learning to sharpen their teaching and partnership strategies, their uninformed strides toward student achievement may act as a brake on their success.

PERSPECTIVES IN A LEARNING COMMUNITY

How is it different to work in a culture of learning and growing (see Figure 2.1)? A learning community has to be shaped by all levels of the organization. Researchers have identified several characteristics of a collaborative school culture with norms and expectations that support change and improvement, including the following:

- Collegiality with peers
- Experimentation in the workplace
- High expectations for self and students
- Trust and confidence in interactions
- Tangible support from administration and peers
- An accessible knowledge base
- Appreciation and recognition, accountability for work
- Caring, celebration, and humor in the workplace
- Involvement in decision making at the governance level
- Protection of what's important in the workplace
- Honest, open communication
- Meaningful traditions (Saphier & King, 1985)

Our experience in working with schools leads us to add the following:

- Mutual respect in the workplace
- Disagreement expressed openly, without rancor
- Regard for professional learning, especially when compiling data for decision making
- Understanding and use of a cycle of inquiry to improve teaching and learning

Experiences in working with teachers also led us to reflect on what many teachers cannot or will not do in a school culture. Teachers are reluctant to close down a current system to start another new one. They don't voluntarily change the culture of a school in which they are experienced, comfortable, and secure. They won't envision, develop, implement, and

Figure 2.1   Perspectives in a Learning Community: How Will It Be Different?

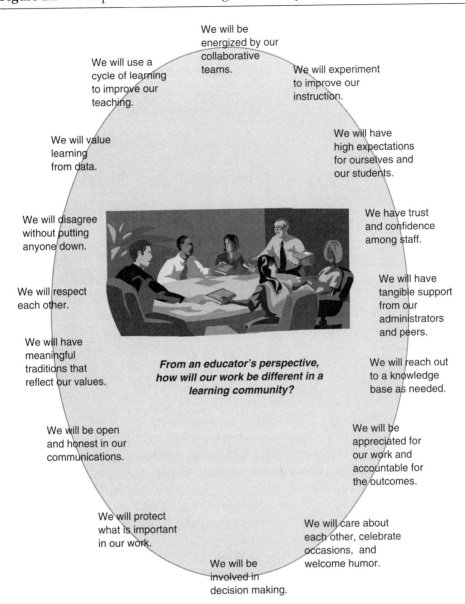

We will be energized by our collaborative teams.

We will use a cycle of learning to improve our teaching.

We will experiment to improve our instruction.

We will value learning from data.

We will have high expectations for ourselves and our students.

We will disagree without putting anyone down.

We have trust and confidence among staff.

We will respect each other.

We will have tangible support from our administrators and peers.

We will have meaningful traditions that reflect our values.

From an educator's perspective, how will our work be different in a learning community?

We will reach out to a knowledge base as needed.

We will be open and honest in our communications.

We will be appreciated for our work and accountable for the outcomes.

We will protect what is important in our work.

We will care about each other, celebrate occasions, and welcome humor.

We will be involved in decision making.

SOURCE: Adapted from the work of Saphier and King (1985).

sustain a new culture until there is support in the system for doing so. Educators must understand how to build a culture of learning in which each member is valued and supported. Ideally, teachers are simultaneously teachers, learners, coaches, and leaders. How effective would our schools be if each member of the school community demonstrated his or her distinct role in successful teaching and learning?

The Role of Leaders in a Learning Culture

What then is the role of the administrator or teacher leader in a learning culture? First, the role of the leader is to put people in touch with their values, the reason they became educators, the reason they chose teaching over business or the other professions, and the reason they are in a school setting with other professional colleagues. Bringing talk about values to the surface is important in a culture. Thomas Sergiovanni (1992) summarizes as follows:

> The evidence seems clear: self-interest is not powerful enough to account fully for human motivation. We are also driven by what we believe is right and good, by how we feel about things, and by the norms that emerge from our connections with other people. (p. 23)

Driven by these values and emerging norms, teachers act in the best interests of students.

Second, a leader must encourage a culture of interactive collaboration and professional networking to be certain even teachers with a history of isolation have opportunities to share and benefit from their colleagues' best thinking. Excellent teachers engage students in high levels of group learning and performance, but most colleagues—some teaching in the same building—do not have the opportunity to observe high-performing classes or to learn from their peers in a professional environment. "If teachers' interests and motivations lie at the heart of successful efforts to enhance classroom practices, then the professional networks that engage teachers comprise promising vehicles for change" (Lieberman & Miller, 1991, p. 78). These networks of support are continuous in a learning community and replace sporadic demonstrations of support that characterized schools in the past.

Third, leaders must model effective listening and learning throughout the organization. If leaders are truly helping students advance in their learning, they must be learner models. Moreover, students need to see how teamwork, collaboration, and action research work for their teachers. As students prepare for multiple careers, they are also preparing for a lifetime of relationships and interactions that would be greatly enhanced by observing their teachers modeling the behaviors that are expected from students. Roland Barth (1990) uses the analogy of an oxygen mask in the airplane. Passengers traveling with small children are instructed to put the oxygen over their own faces first and only then to place the mask on their children's faces. He continues as follows:

> Principals . . . desperately want teachers to breathe in new ideas, yet do not themselves engage in visible, serious learning. Teachers badly want their students to learn to perform at grade level, yet seldom reveal themselves to children as learners. (p. 42)

In a learning community, people of all generations and all positions are teachers and learners, simultaneously, and once they have experienced the difference, there's no turning back.

Fourth, educators are reflectors. They traditionally reflect on their own teaching and student learning, but it may or may not result in a revised curriculum. In a learning community, leaders encourage teachers to share their inquiry and use data in drawing conclusions as their teams focus on how to improve teaching and learning. Teachers use data collected from their use of new strategies to guide curricular revisions. Action research motivates them to try new strategies to improve the achievement of all students, and the support of colleagues in high-performing teams helps to sustain the energy.

Fifth, leaders are concerned about professional growth. Why should this growth be focused on an individual educator? It is far more productive for the growth to be not only continuous but also a norm in the learning community. With common values, faculty and administrators become more comfortable using a cycle of inquiry and action research as they reach out for learning resources to improve their ability to teach all students. Leaders are key in closing the gap from isolated effectiveness of individual staff to schoolwide success (see Figure 2.2).

Figure 2.2   Closing the Gaps to Form a Learning Community

Individual	Learning Community
Isolation	Collaboration
No plan of support	Network of support
Personal success or failure	School success or failure
Personal learning and reflection	Shared inquiry with action research
Struggle with new strategies	Shared strategies and collaborative evaluation
Teacher growth left to the individual	Continuous growth of all teachers
Not affiliated with any team	Member of a high-performing team

FROM ABSTRACT TO CONCRETE

Once we assume that leaders have the idea about how their schools can improve, they must also know when to move their concerns from abstract to concrete. A leader prepares to embark on specific pathways by first being reflective. The leader listens, asks questions, and involves staff in selecting strategies leading to the changes. The leader must then move these thoughts to actions. Knowing his or her responsibilities in pursuing professional development support for a standards-based curriculum, for example, implies that the leader is knowledgeable about the standards as well as about disaggregating data to identify gaps in student learning. Awareness of effective teaching strategies enables leaders to encourage multiple levels of adult and student learning. Differentiated learning, for example, is an excellent strategy when applied to student learning as well as to professional development for staff.

Leaders' effectiveness in determining and securing financial and academic resources may mean the success or failure of their actions. Administrators, district office personnel, and board members are accountable for their allocation of resources. Their accountability must include how the resources will improve student achievement. In education, as in most organizations, human resources are also critical. Leaders should be prepared to identify teacher coaches, support networks, district office personnel skilled in teaching practices, and outside consultants with specific expertise to address expressed needs.

What tools will a leader need to disaggregate data, access technology, promote communications, provide Web access, or ensure meaningful evaluations? The list is endless, but a successful leader listens carefully and determines which tools are needed to provide support. These actions then become evidence of a leader's commitment to the success of students.

In the system are exemplary, as well as defeating, practices. Acknowledging these practices and determining whether or not they are aligned with the vision of improved student achievement is another step in the process. For example, if a faculty is accustomed to having their professional development generated from "experts" outside their school, they probably will not take responsibility for the outcomes. Is this the most effective practice for determining a staff's professional development? This practice needs to be reexamined, and if it doesn't measure up, the practice should be eliminated and a more productive practice put into place. Involving teachers in planning their own high-quality professional development is an accepted practice of successful schools. As a leader shapes the learning community, the need for a thoughtful progression from abstract to concrete will become increasingly evident (see Figure 2.3).

THE ROLE OF TEACHERS IN A LEARNING CULTURE

The role of a teacher in a learning culture is to create a climate of high expectations for teachers and students and a culture of collaboration to achieve the expected levels. Teamwork and collaboration are necessary

Figure 2.3   Concerns of a Leader: From Abstract to Concrete

I believe that . . .	My concrete questions are . . .
I am a leader.	What are my responsibilities?
I must focus my efforts.	What knowledge of data will I need?
Our culture will reflect our goal of student achievement.	What strategies will I use?
Learning will be a priority in all that we do.	What financial and academic resources can I count on to align to our purpose?
This school will work for all students.	What human resources are required?
Technology will help us achieve our goals.	What tools do I need?
Collaboration will enable us to be stronger.	What practices should I institute or continue?

As leaders shape the learning community, the need for a thoughtful progression from abstract to concrete will become increasingly evident.

because the job of an educator in creating and delivering curricula is too difficult to accomplish alone. Teachers need to reevaluate the time they spend working in isolation to prepare for their classes and balance that time with collaborating with more than one professional about how to approach a lesson, a unit, or a standard or how to bolster a student unable to handle the content.

To test our theory about how little many districts currently invest in collaborative activities, we asked teachers in a training seminar to estimate the following:

1. How much time they spent in school preparing for classes in a week

2. How much time they spent outside of school preparing for classes in a week

3. How much time they spent discussing their work with colleagues

4. How much time they spent investing in collaboration, dividing their work among colleagues, and discussing the work they received from other team members

The answers were revealing. When asked how many spent 50% or more of their class preparation time collaborating with colleagues, the number of hands raised in a room of thirty-one teachers was zero. When the question was changed to "How many spend at least 40%, 30%, or 20% of your time collaborating?" still no hands were raised. When the question about the percentage of time dropped to 10% of preparation time in collaboration, four hands raised. All others spent less than 10% of their preparation time collaborating.

How should we have predicted these findings? We could have looked at how these teachers came through the educational system or possibly their struggles with cooperative learning as a teaching strategy. Teachers were embarrassed to admit that they couldn't "control a class" in a cooperative setting. Others resented having to justify giving an excessive number of high grades. How colleagues prepared for teaching, taught integrated units, or assessed learning were often well-guarded secrets. It is not surprising that in 2004, many teachers are still not sharing their successes and challenges, nor are they collaborating to improve student learning.

Teaching has often been referred to as a lonely profession. In fact, Lieberman and Miller (1991) state the following:

> It is no longer necessary to comment on the isolation factor in relation to teaching. For too long, teachers, unlike most other professionals, have been compartmentalized, much like workers in a cottage industry, with few opportunities for meaningful and sustained interactions with one another. (pp. 249–250)

The reality is that the teachers we questioned did not collaborate as a strategy for improved learning or curriculum revision. Did they prefer not to collaborate? Did they not know how to effectively collaborate? Did they have no consistent opportunity to collaborate, as Lieberman and Miller (1991) confirmed in their research? Or did they not value collaboration as a link to classroom effectiveness? Whatever the reason, the conclusions were clear: Collaborations were not a norm in this district, and without an intensive effort and support on the part of the administrators and faculty leaders, the comfortable pattern of isolation established from years of modeling and practice would not be broken. The reasons for teachers to collaborate must be so compelling that teachers will be willing to stretch beyond their paradigm of professional expectations, beyond the boundaries they have set for their collegial involvement.

THE ROLE OF A DISTRICT IN A LEARNING CULTURE

Although the impetus for reform may come from either the school or the district, a culture of reform is not sustainable without support from the district office for professional learning. Nor will the public acknowledge a reformed or successful district without observing significant improvement in student achievement, school by school. Educators are not knowledgeable about how to develop learning communities or how to support reform throughout an entire district. A district that sustains change efforts, in which every school is connecting with all students and all students are meeting standards and demonstrating proficiency, is difficult to find. After more than sixty years of working at the problem of change in schools, we have come to the conclusion that change is peculiarly difficult in schools because the schools and districts lack the capacities needed to support and sustain change efforts. Even in private companies when these support systems are in place, change is difficult; in public school systems, where there is little support, real change seems impossible. Regardless of this observation, educators have not given up on the idea that schools can be, and should be, changed in fundamental ways. If improvements are to occur, however, those who lead must come to understand that to change schools and change what occurs in classrooms, reformers must first ensure that the capacity of the educational system supports and sustains whatever must occur (Schlechty, 1997, pp. 80–81).

Despite numerous examples of "schools that work," few examples can be found of school districts where all the schools work as well as the community would like—exemplary school districts are harder to find than exemplary schools within school districts that seem to be failing. Further, when exemplary districts do appear, they tend to be relatively small or to consist of clusters of schools in larger school districts, such as East Harlem District 4 in New York City, which includes the highly praised Central Park East Secondary School. Indeed, much of the early research on effective schools was based on locating schools that worked inside school districts that did not (Schlechty, 1997, p. 77).

Over the years, national groups have made several attempts to identify the work of boards of education. One of the problems is that when special interest groups elect board members, the interests of the newly elected members are tied to their sponsors instead of student achievement. How often do boards commit to fundamental systems that teachers will continue to learn and students will continue to improve? Single-interest board members who do not set priorities for the district based on the success of all students have frustrated conscientious teachers and administrators. Likewise, when board members demand an increase in student achievement and the improvements are not forthcoming, they too become frustrated with administrators and teachers. The synchronicity of schools and school districts sets the tone for all concerned and is critical if the public is to see improvement in the schools.

THE ROLE OF THE BOARD
IN SUPPORT OF A LEARNING CULTURE

Some boards make courageous decisions to support change efforts in the schools. Seeking to change the culture of the district to become more focused, they use strategic-planning processes as well as district-generated future scenarios to make informed decisions about potential directions for the organization. As a result of the process and new understandings about how to bring about changes in their culture, they institute board policies regarding learning opportunities for students, teachers, and parents of the community.

All reform efforts—adoption of standards and assessment objectives, federal initiatives, state mandates, political change—highlight the need for professional development policies in the district. Included in the policies should be the professional growth of board members—a need that is just as real as the need for teachers, administrators, and classified staff to achieve greater competence in their positions. When boards expand their own capacities to be current, not only with the changes of school populations but also with changes in teaching and learning, they are better prepared to support a districtwide focus on student achievement with professional development dollars for teachers. "We are all learners" is the message they send to every student in the district.

Strategic plans can result in a major thrust in support of a learning community. As teachers revise their district grade-level expectations of students, and as assessments are used to determine whether or not students should be promoted or graduated, boards must continue their support of the goal to educate each student. In one district, the board conducted an extensive informational campaign. A major change in this district was that more parents were drawn into the learning community by becoming aware of the standards and the teachers' expectations that all students will meet the standards. This, in itself, was not sufficient because, although the standards and expectations were in place, the district did not have a plan for supporting teachers to learn strategies to make certain all students could meet the standards. Saying to one student who expects to be promoted or graduated, "You made it," and to another, "You didn't, so try harder next time," is an old way of thinking that supports the theory of sort and select instead of the goal that every student will succeed. In a similar vein, directing faculties to teach all students to meet the standards without asking them what they need to fill the gaps in their own learning is also an invalid approach to reform.

Although learning opportunities can be as varied as the needs of individual schools, everyone must stay focused on the vision. Will district and school administrators be evaluated on their involvement in and support of the board goals? In fact, more administrators are being evaluated on student success at the location of their responsibilities.

COMMUNICATION LINKS
IN A LEARNING COMMUNITY

In a learning community, communications are essential. Teachers who have committed themselves to improving learning communicate that commitment every day. Principals and teacher leaders recognize the importance of keeping each other informed as they build relationships and meet each other's expectations in the difficult work of student achievement.

As board members are elected and as district office staff members are hired, one criterion that is often underestimated is how well each person communicates. Communication links are very complex in a changing system and are vital to the success of the district's support for schools. In forward-looking districts, district offices support every link that the school makes in its restructuring or reforming efforts. In addition, the board of education plays a key role as a vital communication link with the entire community, including the unique communities of individual schools. Once the focus on student achievement has been determined to be the top priority of the district, board members must seize every opportunity to support the schools. When the media interview board members, for example, it is important for the board to weave into the conversation support for change efforts of the schools as well as the focus on student achievement. A board member who is asked about an occurrence of violence in the schools usually responds by describing steps the district is taking to ensure the safety of all students. In the same conversation with media, the next point should always be to recognize steps the district is taking to ensure each student's opportunity for learning, including the continuous preparation of all staff working with students. Taking advantage of such opportunities to support the primary purpose of schooling should be the mental model for each leader in the school community. In one district, board members were asked to frame their monthly reports around the phrase "how I supported student achievement in the schools."

As the superintendent or board members enter the schools, no matter the reason, they should acknowledge the learning that teachers are engaged in to support student achievement of the standards. When board support is low, the work of the schools is impaired. Symbolic actions of top leadership to support teaching and learning are very powerful statements about the direction of the district. Through these vital communication links used in continuous support of student achievement, district leadership will align the actions of the entire district with its purpose (see Figure 2.4).

THE PURPOSE OF PROFESSIONAL
DEVELOPMENT IN A LEARNING CULTURE

From the district and school perspective, the purpose of professional development is to further the achievement of students. The purpose, by definition,

Figure 2.4   Board Support for the Work of Their Schools

When board support for students and schools is low, the goal to improve student achievement is impaired. A high level of commitment is needed for this critical purpose.

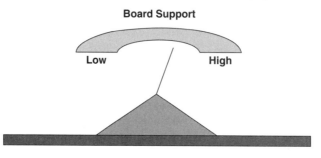

Board Support

Low   High

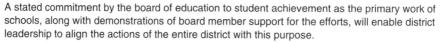

A stated commitment by the board of education to student achievement as the primary work of schools, along with demonstrations of board member support for the efforts, will enable district leadership to align the actions of the entire district with this purpose.

is in concert with the continuous preparation of teachers, who are learning to educate in new ways to raise the achievement level of all students. Needing to show results, a district bases its outcomes on academic needs, with student and teacher learning components. A knowledge base embedded in the school culture is essential for the entire educational community. Regarding this point, Linda Darling-Hammond (1997) stated the following:

> Content must include conceptual knowledge of subject matter; knowledge about children's cognitive, social, and personal development; understanding of learning and motivation; appreciation for the diversity of children's learning experiences and approaches to learning and knowledge of varied teaching strategies to address them; skill in using collaborative learning techniques, new curriculum tools and technologies, and sophisticated assessments of learning and the capacity to work collectively and reflect on practice with other teachers. (p. 334)

Multiple Perspectives

How do we include diverse participants in the design of a learning community to bring multiple perspectives to change efforts? This is a consideration for all professional development efforts. If only experienced teachers are brought into a planning room, for example, the district will lose the perspectives of teachers new to the district. When the planning committees pay attention to the diversity of their members, what they accomplish will be the result of their collective best thinking about students and about how to improve each student's level of achievement.

Notice the difference in perspective. How many district-generated committees in the past have focused on improving the schools or district but have not affected student learning? In districts determined to raise student achievement, superintendents can ill afford scattered approaches to planning professional development in their schools. Such lack of focus wastes precious resources, fiscal and human. Measuring the value of programs means that districts must have a yardstick, and that yardstick is results.

Time for Learning

Time to invest in this process is directly related to the complexities of the tasks. Just as districts cannot demand profound change in a year, on the balance, neither can they afford to wait. Students cannot delay their education while they wait for schools to change. A year in the life of a student is so critical it may be the determiner of whether a student stays in school or drops out, whether he or she pursues an education or is indifferent to it. Will the light of academic understanding and excitement be kindled or suffocated? Students can't wait for changes that will connect them to their schools. Neither can teachers wait for the learning that will sustain their efforts to increase academic achievement. State legislators must hear the impassioned pleas of educators to provide for continuous professional learning, and it is the responsibility of districts and boards to help carry the message.

Evidence of a Learning Community

What is the evidence that educators will produce if they are indeed in a learning community? What actions will identify a staff continuously engaged in learning? Do staff members take individual responsibility for leading analyses of student work? Do they learn from data? Are they comfortable in presenting their findings or conducting seminars with other faculty? Do they use action research based on their data to alter curriculum? Do they put a high value on improved student achievement? Do they discuss professional books, articles, related software, and Web sites? Do they respect and trust all members of the community? Do they interact with diverse perspectives? Are they teachers, learners, coaches, and leaders in a variety of situations?

Interestingly, some claim that schools have always been learning communities. We disagree. Schools are too often filled with private practitioners who infrequently communicate about student learning. In one middle school, the young teachers were so concerned about their isolation in the classroom that they started weekly meetings. They even identified their needs as new teachers by referring to the participants as a support group. The group discussed such questions as "What are the laws regarding a student's right to privacy when a teacher discusses every detail of his learning problems, including his family history, for all staff and guests to hear in the faculty room?" and "Why is talking about diversity in our school a taboo subject? Is it really because 'it isn't an issue' or is it because we don't want to discuss the teacher's role in student failure?" In a learning community, the questions they asked would be placed in front of the entire staff for dialogue and inquiry. In essence, a staff that does not seek opportunities to discuss the big issues of teaching and learning is operating in a learning vacuum.

In some schools, when new concepts are introduced to educators, the unspoken intent of educators is to protect themselves from any learning that might disrupt the way they teach or administer the schools. Conversely, the signs of a learning community are observable to everyone because the processes are deeply embedded in a school's culture. They form evidence of a learning community because they shape the environment in which teachers are learners and also coaches and leaders. The overview presented in Figure 2.5 will help teachers and principals see how these practices can form the culture of the school.

Figure 2.5   Evidence of a Culture of Learning in a Learning Community

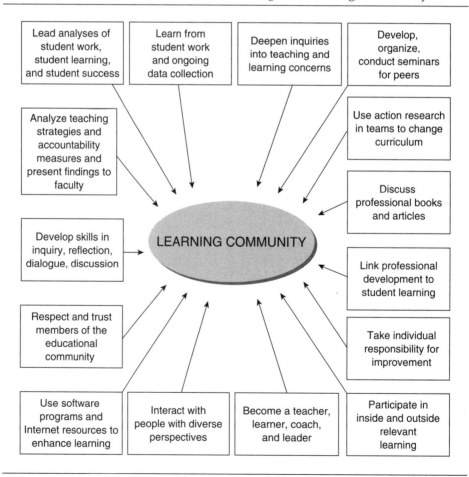

Evidence of a Culture of Learning Survey

How do educators look at their own situations to produce evidence of a culture of learning? They look for actions in their schools that reveal the tremendous energy generated by a staff continuously engaged in learning. Sometimes concepts may be closer than they appear. School leaders can use the Evidence of a Culture of Learning Survey (Table 2.1) as a way to heighten awareness of staff about what it takes to be a successful learning community and how close they are to fulfilling the ideal.

Table 2.1   Evidence of a Culture of Learning Survey

Directions: For each question, circle the number that best represents the answer as it relates to the current professional development program in your school or district based on the scale below.

1	2	3	4
Never	*Seldom*	*Usually*	*Always*

1. Do faculty members lead analyses of student work, student learning, and student success related to the standards?

    1   2   3   4

2. Do faculty members facilitate discussions of teaching strategies and accountability measures and present research findings to faculty and other members of the school community?

    1   2   3   4

3. Is there evidence of the faculty's excellent communication skills in inquiry, reflection, dialogue, and discussion?

    1   2   3   4

4. When teachers use a variety of software programs related to teaching content areas, do they share sources and Web sites to enhance learning on a regular basis?

    1   2   3   4

5. Do teacher leaders have a demonstrated ability to organize, develop, and conduct training for adults? A willingness to provide coaching to peers?

    1   2   3   4

(Continued)

Table 2.1 (Continued)

6. Do teachers feel a shared responsibility for each other's learning?

    1   2   3   4

7. Do faculty members demonstrate the ability to interact with diverse perspectives via telephone, e-mail, and personal contact with all other members of the school community, including classified staff, peer teachers, and administrators as well as parents and other community members?

    1   2   3   4

8. Do teachers engage in action research cycles with their teams to make changes in their curriculum?

    1   2   3   4

9. Do faculty members learn from the study of student work in relation to the standards? Are these learning opportunities quality professional development?

    1   2   3   4

10. Do teachers and administrators exchange and discuss professional articles and book selections? When they are asked to identify and share concepts that will inform their work, do they willingly participate?

    1   2   3   4

11. Do staff members demonstrate that their involvement in quality professional development is a pathway to improved student learning?

    1   2   3   4

12. Do staff members participate in learning opportunities inside and outside the school?

    1   2   3   4

13. Do teachers and administrators participate as teachers, learners, coaches, and leaders?

    1   2   3   4

14. Do teachers and administrators respond to inquiries about teaching and learning in depth or express the need to learn more about professional subjects?

    1   2   3   4

15. Do all educators take individual responsibility for improvement and are educators accountable to the community?

1   2   3   4

16. Do teachers and administrators have respect for and trust all other members of the educational community?

1   2   3   4

Total score: _____ divided by 16 = _____

How does this score inform your professional development design and practices in a learning community?

First, this chapter is not about finite lists. Educators living and working in a learning community could add many more practices. A learning community evolves, just as individuals continue to grow, change, and reshape themselves based on their new learning. A learning community is a natural extension of professional effectiveness for teachers and principals. Educators are aware of the larger system that they need to connect with, but they may not be aware of the advantages of building a learning community that reaches beyond the school grounds to increase student achievement. Educators can experience a tremendous opportunity to walk the talk of education by modeling teaching and learning at every level. There are some challenges to engaging others in a commitment to build a learning community. Principals and teachers have committed their professional energies to increasing student achievement through working with their faculties and their communities to build and sustain a support system for students.

Meeting the challenges of public education is the work of professional educators. When the work is the most challenging, the desire to succeed takes on an intensity that keeps educators moving through the rough times. The work is too important and too challenging for an individual or school to tackle alone. Building a learning community is like weaving a safety net for students that will also catch educators who occasionally waver at the heights of teaching and learning.

Could educators benefit from assistance with the complex tasks involved in teaching and learning? What a tremendous challenge to sift through the extensive new knowledge about teaching strategies, learning patterns, or content-specific information related to standards and at the same time to stay in touch with all the environmental changes that have profound effects on students and their learning. Help is forthcoming in a learning community. Some educators assume that the challenge to reform their schools into learning communities is too great. It is a challenge worth accepting, however, because the consequences of stagnant school communities are too damaging to students and staff.

OUR LEARNING HORIZONS

The philosophy of "do something" may cause some teachers to be incensed when challenged to explain student lack of preparedness to meet grade-level standards. In response to board and parent demands, teachers may cite all the other factors that go into a student's learning as reasons for failure: Socioeconomic conditions, lack of positive parental influence, and lack of preparedness for the next grade level are all given as reasons for future student failure. The accountability part of the challenge is that no educator can assume that one teacher's failure with a student will be remedied at some later time in some other classroom or, worse yet, that it doesn't matter. Before schools had standards in place, middle school teachers may not have been overly concerned that students were failing in high school. With standards, we now see our responsibility for ensuring a student's success no matter where he or she is in the system. Students demonstrate their learning because the schools hold them accountable so that they will enter the next phase of their academic preparation with the skills, knowledge, and performance capability expected of them. When students were passed from one grade level to the next without demonstrated competence, teachers could predict failure at the next level, and they were usually right. When a student's failure to meet standards is directly linked to a teacher's capacity to teach, the need to understand more about teaching and learning, to expand a teacher's horizon, becomes a very high priority for public school teachers, their principals, and their districts. Without continuous opportunities for all teachers to expand their knowledge and skills, schools have little chance of succeeding (Darling-Hammond, 1997, pp. 270–273).

A PARADOX OF VALUES

In reality an individual's personal need for learning is sometimes overshadowed by needs for professional development as perceived by the district office, county, or state. Teachers' needs are suppressed, while prescribed professional development based on assumptions of need are implemented. Conversely, when individuals select their own professional development regardless of the school's needs, a conflict in values emerges. Both individual and schoolwide learning is available in a learning community, and both are focused on improving student learning. It becomes fairly easy for leaders to determine the appropriateness of the professional development when decisions are based on data as well as focus. By considering individual needs along with needs of teams, and involving teachers in the decision making, the leaders are able to target professional development. Consequently, the training becomes more meaningful as teachers accept responsibility for the outcomes.

One team, for example, on examination of data realized that a large percentage of students were not meeting the math standards for estimation. They requested targeted learning and strategies for teaching estimation. Based on the same data, other teams needed professional learning regarding student failure of different standards in the math curriculum. Teacher leaders' research indicated that math coordinators at the county level had an excellent coaching program for various areas of math at their level. By contracting with these consultants to provide training and coaching, and recruiting in-house teachers to assist, they were able to address the concerns of several teams at the school. Individual needs were met along with the needs of the school.

Teachers in one of our classes related that most disturbing of all in their schools and districts was the continuous change of leadership. Nothing seemed to be stable or dependable because the focus kept changing as new leaders entered the system. Other educators reported dissatisfaction in their situations when the systems were so rigid and people so inflexible that teachers had to be in residence for ten years before their voices were heard by the administration. In a learning community, core purposes form the foundation as all teachers explore new approaches to refine and enhance student achievement.

The saying "you can't see the forest for the trees" implies that the big picture is outside our vision and understanding. We might add that neither do we want to see only the forest and forget that it consists of trees, shrubs, flowers, birds, wildlife, and bedrock. From either standpoint, our vision is diminished by what we cannot see. In schools where a teacher focuses just on the data from one class, without seeing the big picture for student success, the entire faculty may be limited from working together to accomplish its goals. Conversely, if educators see only the big picture of student achievement but have little or no understanding of the specific actions needed to produce results, once again they will have brakes on their potential success. Successful educators understand their part in the larger scheme. At the same time, when they value the culture of a learning community, they collaborate with other team members to develop special skills and strategies to improve student learning.

The annual rituals of crisis and denial regarding student assessments usually involve a conversation about time. Time is a major issue in any conversation about school reform. Some teachers view professional time as minutes and hours of their own time to be personally controlled. Some leaders are adamant that professional time belongs to whole-school efforts under their control. In a culture of learning, educators recognize that time is a commodity to be invested in improvement of student achievement. At times that means individual skill building; at other times that means focusing on job-embedded action research for purposes of curricular revision. As teachers become more involved in selecting professional growth opportunities to improve student success, students benefit. It is the function of the leader to shape the learning community by recognizing and confronting dominant values in the organization (see Figure 2.6).

Expectations of Professional Development

A middle school teacher joined a group looking at student work with no designated outcomes. Justifiably so, she wanted to know the purpose of the activity. The response was that they were to look at student work. She and others found it interesting for about five minutes; then they expressed that engaging beyond that was a waste of time. The leaders had failed to establish that looking at student work was a source of data for teachers to improve their teaching. Several weeks later the same group met during time designated for professional development to examine student work and assess it against a standard of performance rubric. She found the process tremendously valuable. What had changed?

The first conversation had no substantive implications for her work; the purpose had not been established. The second conversation directly connected her to the effectiveness of teaching by questioning if students had achieved an acceptable level of performance aligned to the content standard. She began to analyze her own work: "What did I do that helped students achieve the standard? How was I more or less effective for students? What is the evidence?" Everything in her language arts classes came under scrutiny—homework, field trips, library help classes, research projects, critical essays, participation in plays, interpretation of poetry. The strategies were now focused on the results—achieving the standards. When she was able to analyze the data and scrutinize her own as well as her team's performance, she was also able to determine that she needed to improve her personal effectiveness. When she met with colleagues to analyze student performance across grade levels, she was looking for specific information. As she returned to her team, her concerns changed from "What do I have to attend this year for my professional development credits?" to "I need to target critical thinking and expository writing as my

Figure 2.6   The Paradox of Values in a Learning Community

First Value Dominates	Second Value Dominates	A Learning Community
An individual has a personal need for learning.	The school decides the learning suppresses an individual teacher's needs.	Both individual and schoolwide learning is available in the learning community.
Change is constant and nothing seems stable or dependable. Learning opportunities are unconnected.	Systems are rigid and inflexible. Learning is stagnated.	Core purposes provide the foundation as teachers explore new approaches to refine and enhance student learning.
Focus on personal class data prevents teachers from seeing the big picture. Teachers are absorbed in the minutiae, forgetting the goals for student success.	Broad views of student achievement dominate with little understanding of specific actions needed to bring results.	Educators understand their part in the larger scheme while collaborating to develop special skills that improve student learning.
Teachers consider professional time as their personal time over which they have control.	School leaders are adamant that professional time belongs to whole-school efforts.	Educators recognize that time is a commodity to be invested in improvement of student achievement.

SOURCE: Adapted from Ramsey (1997).

greatest needs for professional development this year." She later suggested to her team, "Why don't we all consider professional learning in these areas, especially since students across our grade level are weak in their performances of the standards?"

Perhaps wisely avoiding the notion of being outdated, successful educators have shifted from their view of students as passive recipients of classroom instruction to a concern with what schools must do to help students learn and be successful. In a student-centered school, the focus, obviously, is student learning. Teachers will not be afraid to confront these new challenges within the culture of a learning community. They will be willing to enhance their professional reputations by trying something new.

Based on their experiences with a learning community, teachers know that they will be supported and encouraged to take risks on behalf of students, even if not all ventures are successful.

Where to Be Fluid and Where to Hold Fast

School faculties must be like high-performing teams—certain of the goal, focused on the outcome, aware of every member's role, confident of others' skills as well as their own, willing to learn from data, trusting themselves and others to do their jobs, and confident that, with all the teams working together, students will succeed. No one is immune to such scrutiny. The culture must reflect and support these qualities so that high-performing teams can accomplish their purpose.

So where are we fixed in concrete? Educators must acknowledge that professional learning is what they are about. To increase their effectiveness with students, they are willing to close the gaps of their own learning. They continue to work toward a culture of learning and leading at every level. And where are they fluid? Teacher teams should be free to assess their professional development needs based on student performance and schoolwide data. They are encouraged to search for professional development content and strategies that align with their goals while meeting the needs and goals of the school and district. In essence, once the goal is agreed on, teachers play a key role in determining the learning pathways they will take to accomplish the goal. They are also willing to be accountable for their learning and to demonstrate the impact on student success. The culture of continuous learning and improvement is essential to public education professionals and the students they serve.

Rapidly, it becomes obvious to readers of educational reform initiatives that districts and schools must hold fast on the improved performance of students and the improved effectiveness of teachers. Failure to organize a district around raising student achievement is to ignore the public's mandate for its schools. High expectations for all students are revealed in the district's adopted standards and assessments, which require a demonstration of performance to meet the standards. How do educators teach to the standards? How do they embed standards in the curriculum? What strategies do they learn to expand their capacities to help students meet the standards? How do they report student progress to their unique or collective communities? These are the fluid decisions for individual schools and districts to make.

What will it take for performance levels of large numbers of students to reach the standards? To make a performance-based system effective, the school—indeed, the school district because policies are in effect districtwide—needs to transform the system to ensure that students succeed. It needs to provide additional help to students who are falling behind. It needs to provide high-quality professional development to teachers to enable them to teach students in ways that will ensure that they can meet standards. It needs to reorganize the organization and management of the school so that the principal and teacher leaders make decisions based on what students need to reach the standards. It needs to redirect resources so that the resources are concentrated on strategies that enable the school to achieve the desired results. It needs to engage parents and the public to support high standards for all students (Marsh & Codding, 1999, p. 17). Building a culture of learning and achievement is foremost.

It is no surprise that students in classes of fifty or sixty are tired of waiting until teachers can get around to helping them. Students are dropping out because they are not connecting to what their instructors are teaching or to how they are facilitating student learning. Districts will be forced to learn how students are processing information and how they are connecting their learning to a foundation of experiences as they struggle to make meaning. If there is a message in books from the business world to educators, it is that instructors must learn to be far more flexible in varying teaching strategies and recognizing the fluidity of how each student learns. If, for example, one strategy isn't working, do teachers have a second, third, or fourth teaching strategy, or do they partner students with mentors who can help them immediately? This is a now generation. For some students, if a few minutes of scanning the materials don't produce an answer, they give up because neither the search nor the outcome is worth the time and effort. In essence, school staffs must continuously increase their effectiveness in teaching students how to learn, how to process information, and what to do when students become frustrated with the complexities. Teacher effectiveness is the key to a student's success (Darling-Hammond, 1997); therefore, districts must help teachers continuously expand their knowledge about content, processes, and professional strategies with high-quality professional development and an active community of learning so that they are equipped to teach in this connected world. Teachers can be fluid in how they teach, but districts, in response to the public, will hold fast to the premise that all students will be academically successful and will have the data to prove their results.

CONCLUSION

Will each professional involved in the public schools make a commitment to caring relationships, conscious valuing, and the academic success of all students? Will imagination, intellectual drive, curiosity, and a desire for success be exhibited daily by students, as well as by the adults involved with them? Considering the complex world we live in, the answer to both questions must be affirmative. Teachers, principals, and all other staff involved with students will be empowered to create the best possible environment for student learning and student success. By modeling the very academic and social behaviors they expect students to exhibit, teachers demonstrate commitment to the culture of a learning community that will result in an optimal climate for student success.

At times, districts get caught in a web of political agendas. One member of the school board wants to repave the playgrounds in all the elementary schools. One wants to release a particular administrator. Another has been elected by the teachers' union to represent the financial interests of teachers. And so it goes. One concept is very clear: Unless the district focuses on improved student learning and assesses how every action affects student success, members of the public will become more dissatisfied with the schools they support with tax dollars and, as they are already doing, will seek alternatives. Teachers and principals cannot change schools working alone. They must have support. The time is right for districts to rethink how they have operated in the past and to open themselves to communitywide collaborative actions focused on student success. Teachers and administrators must be prepared to find new ways of connecting with students to enable them to be successful, and at the same time they must commit to continuous improvement of their own skills. Professional growth is part of the question about how educators do "it," and high-quality professional development that includes teachers and principals in the planning process is part of the answer. How will schools and districts grow to meet the challenges of the new century? They will grow through collaborative, articulated, comprehensive, and resource-sufficient professional development programs in the context of a learning community.

Stop and reflect on these key points and their meaning for student achievement in your school.

KEY POINTS

- When the culture of an organization is collaborative, as in a learning community, each teacher has a built-in network of support.
- Collaboration is evidence of both faculty strength and a healthy school climate.
- An important step is to formalize professional development policies that include collaborative interaction as part of any new learning.
- Researchers have identified several characteristics of a collaborative school culture with norms and expectations that support change and improvement.

- The role of leaders in a learning culture is key to closing the gap from isolated effectiveness of individual staff to schoolwide success.
- As a leader shapes the learning community, the need for a thoughtful progression from abstract to concrete becomes increasingly evident.
- The role of teachers in a learning culture is to create a climate of high expectations for teachers and students and a culture of collaboration to achieve the expected levels.
- The reasons for teachers to collaborate must be so compelling that teachers will be willing to stretch beyond their paradigm of professional expectations, beyond the boundaries they have set for their collegial involvement.
- When board support for the schools is low, the work of the schools to improve student achievement is impaired.
- Principals and teacher leaders recognize the importance of communication links as they build relationships and meet professional expectations in the difficult work of student achievement.
- The signs of a learning community are observable to everyone because the processes are deeply embedded in a school's culture. Take the survey to determine your school's effectiveness as a learning community.
- It is the function of the leader to shape the learning community by recognizing and confronting the dominant values of the organization.
- School faculties must be like high-performing teams—certain of the goal, focused on the outcome, aware of every member's role, confident of others' skills as well as their own, willing to learn from data, trusting of themselves and others to do their jobs, and confident that, with all the teams working together, students will succeed.

3

Conditions and Processes for Professional Development

SCENARIO

The leadership team is meeting with the principal to discuss this year's professional development plan. The entire team is wondering what is really needed to improve student learning.

Maria: *How many days do we have for professional learning this year?*

Gilberto: *What do you mean? Days of listening to experts or actual learning?*

Principal: *Those aren't mutually exclusive so long as there is some follow-up to whatever we are doing.*

Frank: *What about the professional development credits we get by doing the cycle of learning and action research? We learn so much by analyzing what our students are doing and trying to figure out what we need to help them.*

Maria: *Well, those aren't actual "days."*

Frank: *Who said we need "days"? Maybe that's an outdated way of looking at professional development.*

Gilberto: *So what is professional development to you?*

Based on your learning and experience, how would you and your colleagues respond to Gilberto's question?

ESSENTIAL QUESTION

What conditions and processes using cycles of improvement (inquiry) will be used to address high-quality professional development focused on student achievement while addressing teacher, team, and school concerns?

Pause for a moment to reflect on this essential question.

IMPORTANCE OF TEACHER CONCERNS FOR PROFESSIONAL DEVELOPMENT

As teachers continue learning to improve the curriculum, instruction, and assessment for increased student achievement, their work concerns must be met in the design of professional development programs (conditions and processes). Teachers should see professional development not as a district mandate but, more important, as effectively embedded in their daily lives, providing continuous professional growth opportunities (Bull & Buechler, 1996; Lieberman & Miller, 2001). The traditional professional development model of onetime training workshops delivered by an outside expert with no follow-up is outdated. In fact, it never was an effective approach to adult learning. A broader and more complex approach to professional development needs to encompass ongoing sustained research, reflection, analysis of data, discussion, peer coaching, mentoring, collaborative planning, problem solving, and involvement in decision making by teachers.

As a district addresses teachers' work concerns and makes professional development plans to incorporate those concerns, it recognizes teachers and validates the importance of their needs, including the conditions and processes used. The issue of their work concerns must influence the planning process and professional learning activities as they are developed. Recognizing and dealing with these concerns in professional development planning allows teachers to participate, take ownership, and understand the purpose. Teachers need professional development that has a coherent focus rather than fragmented activities with little meaning for actual application in the classroom to improve student learning. Shanker (1990) captures the importance of why we should address teacher work concerns in the following statement:

> Every teacher in America's public schools has taken inservice courses, workshops, and training programs. But as universal as the practice has been, so is the disappointment among teachers and management as to the usefulness of most staff development experiences. (p. 91)

Why does this type of professional development practice continue to be perpetuated in our schools and districts? How can we better address teacher work concerns in context with professional development planning and improving student achievement?

Professional development of teachers is central to successful educational reform. The numerous educational reforms facing teachers daily in the classroom include new curricula and instructional strategies; rigorous academic standards for all students; use of multiple measures of student achievement (i.e., standardized tests, portfolios, and performance-based assessments); diversity of student needs (disabilities, languages, cultures, and experiences); technology uses in the classroom; and the new demands of site-based management. Teachers need numerous opportunities and the means to learn new approaches to stay professionally current. Professional development must provide the learning that teachers need to improve instruction, meet student needs, and accelerate achievement. Approaching professional development through the lens of teacher work concerns encourages the designers to collaborate with teachers. As they gain a broader perspective of teachers' needs, professional development designers will begin to validate the relationship between professional development and increased student achievement. Helping teachers expand their repertoire of content knowledge and strategies is meaningful professional growth in the context of teachers' working conditions and concerns.

Researchers have reached a clear consensus that onetime workshops for teachers are ineffective. The content is not transferred to the classroom, nor does it affect student achievement (Joyce & Showers, 1995; Lieberman & Miller, 2001). Instead of sporadic, fragmented workshops, professional development must move beyond the current series of teacher-training workshops to embedding ongoing professional development in the daily work of teachers (Lieberman & Miller, 1999). Opportunities for learning, observation, practice, feedback, coaching, and reflection on practice need to be integrated parts of a teacher's work. Using systems thinking helps us understand that the school should be the focus of professional development, where teachers interact with each other and as teams around issues of learning and achievement and the district supports the site focus in numerous ways. Districts must know how to address the unique challenges of a school site to meet teachers' and students' unique learning needs. When professional development at the site level is tied to a school improvement plan, teachers and administrators can implement a coherent program that takes into consideration their particular needs and how these needs will be addressed.

For a better understanding of research and practices centered on teacher work concerns in relation to professional development, three major areas of concern need to be addressed: roles and responsibilities, conditions of professional development, and processes for professional development.

ROLES AND RESPONSIBILITIES

In the past, school employees had the luxury of assuming that most professional development responsibilities belonged to someone else. Principals and teachers could look to a central office staff member who planned, coordinated, and sometimes even presented professional development programs. Whatever the case, it was possible for virtually all district employees to view professional development as someone else's job.

Today, the concept of job-embedded staff development has come to mean that educators in many roles—superintendents, assistant superintendents, curriculum supervisors, principals, and teacher leaders, among others—must all see themselves as teachers of adults and must view the development of others as one of their most important responsibilities (Lieberman & Miller, 2001; Sparks & Hirsh, 1997, p. 83).

If professional development is focused at the school level so that teachers can meet classroom improvement targets, the roles and responsibilities for teachers must evolve from isolation in their classrooms to involvement in the larger schoolwide view of improvement and professional development. Recognizing the individual roles of teachers in the larger school organization has proven to be critical for schools to reform and improve (Elmore, 1996). Researchers have found that teachers' individual efforts, in random isolation, have not provided the power to move student achievement and school improvement in significant ways (Darling-Hammond & McLaughlin, 1995). Nor have district-level initiatives that vary from year to year made a consistent impact on schools, teachers, and student achievement (Little, 1993a).

Professional development must consistently focus on an overall vision and plan for school improvement that both teachers and administrators understand and make a commitment to carry out. Even the process of developing a coherent vision is itself a form of professional development. Expanding the roles and responsibilities of teachers in professional development will be key to future student success and to the ongoing growth of teachers. Ownership of their own professional development is an important step for teachers in both their roles and responsibilities to the profession. The study of governance issues in professional development by Joyce, Murphy, Showers, and Murphy (1989) confirmed that professional development programs jointly governed (by individual staff, schools, and the district) were considered valuable by educators because involvement and decisions were democratic.

Currently, teachers may be offered a broad range of professional development activities by the district's professional development department in a "buffet style"—a series of workshops that have no clear focus for teachers' professional growth needs or key school improvement goals. In the traditional model of professional development, the role of the teacher is usually as a passive participant or sometimes as a presenter of activities at a workshop. How often have we heard the following: "The district organizes professional development, and we don't go because it is not relevant to where we are and what our needs are." The evolving vision of professional development requires multiple roles for the teacher. Teachers should be designers, leaders, and presenters as well as participants in professional development (Lieberman & Miller, 1999). McLaughlin (1994) emphasized that meaningful professional development takes place not during workshops and inservice presentations but in the context of professional communities that have been locally developed to be responsive to teachers' needs. Successful professional development is no longer the domain of a district-level supervisor; instead, it is organized to give teachers the authority and resources to take charge of their own learning (Little, 1993b).

Expanding the roles of teachers in professional development processes will include increased attention to their roles as school learning community members, teacher leaders, and coaches. These new roles, their responsibilities, and what they entail will recognize teachers, their expertise, and their ability to lead and share professionally to expand teachers' capacity to help students achieve (Lieberman, 1995). Each of these roles will be discussed for its significance.

School Learning Community Team Member

Site-based professional development involves expanding the role of the classroom teacher as a team member of the larger school learning community. As learning community team members, teachers must see their roles and their professional development integrated into support of the overall school improvement plan. The ownership of responsibility for professional development is at the school site level, where specific problems, needs, and possibilities are understood. It only makes sense that teachers involved in the design of their own professional development programs will meet their unique school and student needs (Little, 1993b). As active members of the school learning community, teachers can make professional development an ongoing part of the overall school improvement plan so that it is aligned with both school and district goals (McLaughlin, 1994). Teachers will see the emerging coherence of professional development tied to the school plan and to the work of the school learning community as evidence of a focused, not fragmented, effort. As a member of the school learning community, each teacher has a role in helping the school keep its focus and carry out its goals for student success. As a school learns together in professional development settings, teachers and principals must agree that their focused efforts to study, learn, implement, reflect, and refine practices will result in improved student achievement (Lieberman & Miller, 1999).

Within a school's learning community, the individual professional growth of teachers will still be present and supported as long as these individual opportunities are seen as aligned with the larger plan for school learning and improvement. As teachers engage with colleagues in planning, discussing, practicing, reflecting, and sharing through professional development activities, their concerns about relevant, meaningful professional learning will be addressed. There are multiple ways for teachers to collaborate and learn in professional development settings (small groups, grade-level teams, faculty meetings, and connections to outside subject matter state and national networks and professional associations) to inform their practice.

The point of school-based professional development is that the needs of each school, as defined by the staff at that school, play a major role in determining the form professional development will take. The school is the starting point for professional development planning, not a fortress with unbreachable walls (Bull & Buechler, 1996, p. 9).

Thus, as learners and colleagues within a school learning community, teachers help shape their own professional growth and view it as continuous growth in professional practice based on their unique circumstances and needs. The learning community nurtures teachers' inquiry into their practices and challenges and supports them to improve their practices to achieve student success.

Teacher Leader

Teachers will take on new instructional leadership roles with professional development as members or chairpersons of school improvement site councils or at the district level as members of school improvement teams, expert presenters, teacher leaders, coaches, facilitators, mentors, and problem solvers. Teacher leadership roles may be formal or informal, but it is important that teachers accept and seek leadership roles as professionals taking responsibility for what is happening in the teaching profession and that they value their own ongoing professional learning in the larger context as well as at their schools.

Teachers must share in the leadership role of determining professional growth rather than attending sessions imposed on them by others. Teachers may choose to use outside consultants and experts to help initiate or guide change efforts at their school, or they may capitalize on the expertise of teachers within their own school or district. Even mandated legislation should include shared leadership between teachers and administrators to determine the implementation of the how's and when's of their professional development. Participation in leadership roles demonstrates a collaborative leadership process that gives teachers structured opportunities to participate in decision making. Further, such participation models democratic shared leadership and decision making, which build ownership and commitment for teachers in a school improvement process. "Teachers who are leaders lead within and beyond the classroom, influence others toward improved educational practice, and identify with and contribute to a community of teacher leaders" (Katzenmeyer & Moller, 1996, p. 6). Teachers, as leaders, enact their beliefs daily through their interactions with other teachers, students, parents, and the principal. Leaders must clearly communicate their expectations and voice their strong beliefs about children and schooling. "Principals and teachers in schools that are in the midst of change are finding that as they do their work, they are blurring boundaries and forging new connections between leading, learning, and teaching. Their schools are leadership dense organizations" (Lieberman & Miller, 1999, p. 46). The ideal is that teacher leadership becomes so embedded in a school that when a principal leaves, teacher leaders are able to carry on the change process and provide continuity to the work. The principal can cultivate a culture of teacher leadership by listening, engaging, and empowering teachers to deal with professional learning concerns. In doing this, a principal sends a clear message that teacher concerns matter and that teacher knowledge and experience count. In small steps, the foundation for new forms of leadership in schools can be constructed. Principals must always be attentive to the learning needs of both students and teachers. In collaboration with the faculty, they provide a wide variety of opportunities for growth and development. Every teacher must have the opportunity to learn, and learning can be led by people other than the principal or outside experts. As districts give more leadership and decision-making authority to teachers, an important, untapped leadership resource will be released for improved student learning. The old paradigm of deciding in an administrative vacuum what is good for teachers does not work. Teachers as professionals need and want to be leaders and participants in their own professional learning and growth.

Coach

The teacher's role as coach has emerged as a powerful means of individual and school organizational development. The importance of using teacher coaching as a follow-up to new learning has increased the implementation of new concepts and strategies by teachers. The ongoing coaching support has definitely led to improved student achievement. Teacher as coach makes the theory, demonstration, practice, and feedback elements to support growth more meaningful because they come from a peer as ongoing support for the new learning and application in the classroom. Educators have all experienced how difficult change can be. Even with the best intentions, new information and strategies get filed away for possible future use unless coaching support takes place. The support of a teacher in the role of coach increases individual teacher's or teacher teams' use of new learnings by 85%. The research by Joyce and Showers (1995) substantiates the importance of coaching and feedback and demonstrates that the level of use of new learnings by teachers in their classrooms depends on the type of training procedures used by the coaches. Table 3.1 shows the relationship between types of professional development strategies used and the level of impact on concept understanding, skill attainment, and application by teachers.

Teachers as coaches are able to increase their understandings of the use of skills within their classrooms. Coaching allows teachers to observe each other; give feedback and support; share ideas, lessons, and materials; discuss problems and concerns; and develop curricula together. The isolation of the individual classroom is broken down because professional development through coaching can happen during school hours. Training of coaches can be done by an outside expert, but a cadre of schoolteacher coaches can train new coaches and share the coaching role. Coaches claim they learn as much about teaching as the teachers they coach (Joyce & Showers, 1995). The reflection and discussion of classroom observations allow both the teacher and the coach to reflect on teaching practices and to hone their skills to improve instruction for students. The coach's follow-up of the learning activities reinforces new learnings and also models correct implementation within the classroom. Time is needed for teachers to absorb and practice new ideas or strategies and adapt them to their classrooms. Teachers as coaches help reinforce and refine the new knowledge and sustain the professional development change process for the teacher.

Sparks's (1986) study of professional development activities on the performance of teachers helps substantiate the importance of teacher peer coaching. The study looked at the effects of three types of professional development activities on the performance of teachers: workshops alone, workshops plus coaching by the trainer, and workshops plus peer coaching. The research found that teachers who were coached by peers improved more than those who were coached by experts and that both improved more than teachers who attended workshops alone. Sparks came to the following conclusions regarding teacher peer coaching experiences:

Table 3.1   Level of Impact of Professional Development

Professional Development Type	Level of Impact		
	Concept Understanding	Skill Attainment	Application
Presentation of theory	85%	15%	5%
Modeling	85%	18%	5–10%
Practice and feedback	85%	80%	10–15%
Coaching	90%	90%	80–90%

SOURCE: Adapted from the research of Joyce and Showers (2002).

Teachers rarely get to see one another in action, and just watching a colleague teach may have been a powerful learning experience.

Peer coaches had to analyze the behavior of other teachers, which may have helped them analyze their own behavior more accurately.

Structured interactions with other teachers may have led to a heightened sense of trust and esprit de corps.

It is interesting to note that Joyce and Showers (1995, 2002), in their most recent research, have reversed their definition of *coach*. The coach is the teacher, not the observer, and the observer is learning from the teacher—not observing the teacher for feedback, but learning from the observed teacher and reflecting on his or her own practice. Joyce and Showers explained that they no longer include formal feedback as a component of peer coaching; instead, they emphasize other aspects of peer coaching in peer study teams, where the primary activity is the collaborative planning and development of curriculum and instruction in pursuit of shared goals. Their research raises questions about what feedback means in the coaching process, but their work reinforces the importance of the interaction of collaboration and learning opportunities of peers around their teaching activities.

Understanding these new roles and responsibilities for teachers within the creation of professional development designs is critical. Teachers and their work concerns cannot be ignored because teachers are the vital links between students and learning. Expanding teachers' roles and responsibilities helps expand the participation of teachers in defining their own professional development, thus making teaching more of a profession.

CONDITIONS FOR PROFESSIONAL DEVELOPMENT

Teacher work concerns usually focus on the conditions under which professional development is provided. Questions about time, trust and collaboration, incentives and recognition, resources, leadership, and policies arise when teachers view professional development plans and opportunities (see Figure 3.1). These important conditions for professional development raise questions that should be addressed in designing and meeting the conditional requirements for high-quality professional development:

Will the training be worth my time preparing for a substitute and the time lost with my students?

Who says we have to attend the training and why?

How relevant is the training to my classroom and students? Is it all theory, or are there practical applications?

Will the strategies work in my classroom, and how will I have time to prepare to use my new knowledge and strategies?

What incentives or recognition can I expect, or is it expected that I will do this above and beyond my classroom duties?

What resources and materials are available after the training to help me implement the new knowledge in the classroom?

Who is providing the leadership and follow-up to the professional development?

Which current policies promote high-quality professional development opportunities?

LEADERSHIP AND POLICY

"Staff development that improves the learning of all students requires skillful school and district leaders who guide continuous instructional improvement" (National Staff Development Council, 2001, p. 2). Leadership and advocacy for continuous learning are critical to the professional development and maintenance of an effective school. Only if professional development is embedded in the philosophy, leadership, and organizational structure of schools and districts can a culture of continuous growth thrive (Loucks-Horsely et al., 1987). Leadership and policy coherence can keep schools from being inundated with conflicting demands as they strive to improve and focus their professional development efforts (Little, 1993b). Ideally, school, district, and state improvement plans are coordinated into a seamless

Figure 3.1   Conditions for Professional Development

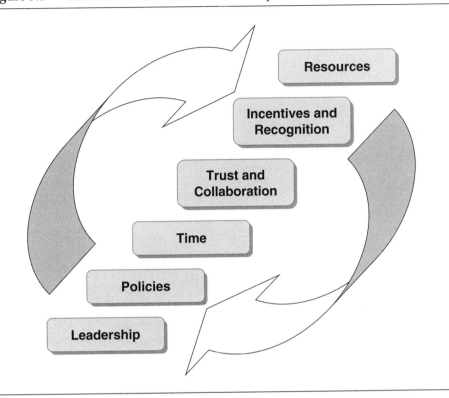

whole, targeted at increasing student learning. Equally important are the district's infrastructure of policies and its commitment of leadership to support continued professional development for teachers. School board policies are enacted to facilitate school-based improvement and to eliminate barriers to professional development. Teachers clearly understand the impact of these district policies and leadership actions on professional development plans. They are tangible evidence of how important professional growth is among district priorities.

It is important for leaders of a district to view continuous professional growth as essential to district and school goals to raise student achievement levels. As an integral part of any district's strategic plan, school boards should enact policies and standards to promote ongoing, quality professional development (Darling-Hammond & McLaughlin, 1995). These policies will provide a guide for planning and implementing new strategies to increase student learning. Policies must create significant roles for teachers in many areas of practice that have previously been managed by others, including setting standards, developing curricula and assessments, and evaluating practices.

Further, policies must focus on stimulating the environment that nurtures high-quality learning communities of teachers, rather than on particular institutional structures and processes. Policymakers should focus on the richness and relevance of the variety and means for teachers to learn in the context of their school environment (Darling-Hammond & McLaughlin, 1995). The leadership and policy environment of a district send a clear message to teachers and should be examined as evidence that districts have, or don't have, high expectations for school improvement.

Time

Reforms conducted on the fringes of the school day will never become an integral part of the school (Purnell & Hill, 1992). In talking with teachers, we found that adequate time for professional development is one of their chief concerns. Time to be involved in professional development training, discussions, decision making, study or task groups or teams, action research inquiry, and collaboration draws the teacher. When, on top of the regular school day schedule and the time needed to correct homework and plan lessons for the next unit, will it be done? How can teachers find time for continuous professional development and learning when their normal days are consumed with all their demanding teaching responsibilities? Time needs to be scheduled for teachers to work together. Individual teachers may take summer or semester courses or workshops, but these are separate, discrete activities based on the individual teacher's motivation and use of personal time. Schools must structure time for professional learning within the regular school calendar, or they must expand the school calendar, if teachers are to have quality time for professional development.

What are the options available for increasing professional development time for teachers and meeting their work concerns? Research and proven practice provide several models for reallocating time within the existing school calendar or by expanding the school year and calendar. Each possible option is briefly discussed in the following sections: accumulated or banked time, alternative grouping, alternative scheduling, expanded staffing, school-university partnerships, expanded professional development hours and days, and expanded school calendar and year.

Accumulated or Banked Time. Increasing instructional minutes during the week to accumulate or bank release minutes can be used as a block of time each week for professional development. Some states require waivers to implement this strategy. Schools using banked time have developed effective block time each week or month to do substantial intense professional development work with their teachers.

Alternative Grouping. Working with colleagues, teachers bring students together in large groups rather than single classes to provide free time for designated teachers. Team teaching, regularly scheduled assemblies, or community service learning offer the means to free teachers and to expand the time available for professional development.

Alternative Scheduling. Altering the master schedule to give teams of teachers common planning time for professional development and collaboration is another action a principal can take to provide quality time. This alternative scheduling can be done under different configurations, such as common planning time at the start or end of the day; use of block scheduling, with teacher-scheduled prep periods; and the addition of an extra period to the schedule so that blocks of time can be available at different times of the day for different teams of teachers.

Expanded Staffing. A school can use regular substitute teachers to free teachers to work on their professional development during the school day. This may include the use of a floating substitute who can move from class to class within a school, releasing teachers for observations, coaching, mentoring, or other types of job-embedded professional development activities. This floating substitute should be a regular who knows the curriculum and students well enough to carry on regular learning activities in the classroom while the teacher is involved in professional development. Another way to expand staff is for administrators to occasionally volunteer to release teachers as a demonstration of clear support for their professional development work. Administrative leaders who help expand staff time for important work by substituting in the classroom also learn themselves by teaching and participating in learning with the students in the classroom.

School-University Partnerships. This approach is very comprehensive and allows for university students or faculty to cover teachers' classrooms. Professional development activities tied to school-university partnerships inform teachers and university practice in a reciprocal way, as those involved share university research and classroom practice. Teachers, student teachers, and university faculty work together on teaching and learning issues that expand their knowledge and abilities. These types of partnerships play an enriching role for both the school and the university in a systematic way.

Expanded Professional Development Hours and Days. Districts can extend the teachers' contracts to include additional hours or days for professional development. The extended contract buys time during the summer for workshops, seminars, curriculum development, and planning, and during the school year the contract adds hours for follow-up. It also buys time for coaching and collaboration, providing the needed time for learning and concept implementation for teachers. Collaboration time for purposes of writing curricula and refining assessment strategies is also an excellent investment for schools.

Expanded School Calendar and Year. The option of expanding the school calendar should be explored more extensively than it has been to date because it could provide quality time for professional development without having teachers leave their classrooms and students. More districts and schools should explore the use of a single-track year-round calendar that shortens the summer vacations and expands periodic breaks during the school year; these breaks can then be used for professional development activities (see Figure 3.2).

The other benefit of the single-track, year-round calendar—besides teachers' professional development—is increased learning for students. It is an important recognition of the amount of learning loss students experience over the summer. Learning loss is less for students with shorter summer breaks (Cooper, Nye, Charlton, Lindsay, & Greathouse, 1996). In addition, teachers use less time reteaching material or establishing classroom management when students have not had an extended three-month summer break from learning and school. The single-track calendar illustrated in Figure 3.2, with periodic breaks and a shorter summer break, could be used for professional development. Continuous learning for teachers and students is better served by a single-track, year-round calendar than the traditional school calendar. The traditional school calendar has its roots in our agrarian history, when students worked in the fields to harvest crops. Educators should take a serious look at the school calendar year and how it is used. Finding the time for continuous professional development over the entire year is a strong possibility in a revised school calendar year.

Given all of these considerations for the use of time for professional development, educators are reminded that there are constraints to be negotiated in the change process. The legislature, the state department of education, the teachers' union (including bargaining agreements), the school board and community, and district policies are all fluid parts of a changing system. The use of time must be addressed if teachers are to transform schools and learning for students (National Commission on Time and Learning, 1994). Time is an essential factor in turning schools into continuous learning communities. If educators and boards refuse to tackle alternative schedules, they are stuck with what they have had in the past: periodic, shallow, or episodic professional development activities that have little or no sustaining effect on a teacher's practice in the classroom.

Time is an important element for continuous learning. Adequate time for professional learning must be allotted. Teachers may be required by their state to take a certain number of professional development hours to renew their teaching licenses, or they may earn salary increases for taking college units or advanced degrees. This is a catch-as-catch-can system. The patchwork nature of this model of professional development will have to change. Continuous learning opportunities must become part of teachers' everyday working lives and part of every school's institutional priorities.

Figure 3.2   Traditional Versus Year-Round Calendar

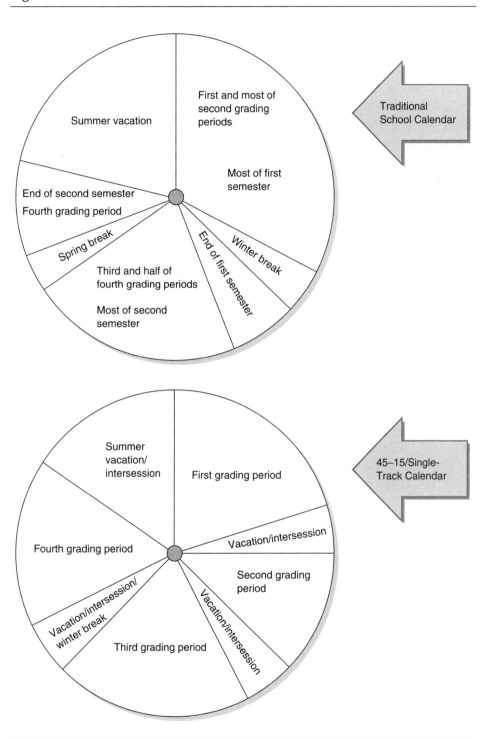

Administrators and teachers will have to develop an ethos of inquiry, as Bull and Buechler (1996) described:

> Examining their own practices and trying new ones;
>
> Learning about subject matter, instructional methods, and student development;
>
> Questioning what they learn in light of their own experience;
>
> Thinking deeply about overall school improvement; and
>
> Working together to enact that improvement. (p. 22)

Time is the critical element that must be provided if these things are to happen.

Trust and Collaboration

Trust and collaboration are hallmark conditions that must be present for learning communities to develop and for teachers to grow, but these are not easy conditions to establish. Most schools are organized in ways that isolate teachers so that collaboration is not easily established or sustained. Working within their classrooms on a daily basis with students, teachers do not have a lot of time for interacting with colleagues or developing trust with other teachers and administrators. Teachers' experiences and their collective understanding of trust and collaboration vary. The skills associated with continuous collegial interactions must be nurtured within the school. Professional development, like school reform efforts in general, works best as a collaborative effort when teachers, administrators, classified staff, students, and parents trust one another and can work together over a sustained period of time.

As schools become learning communities, trust and collaboration are developed and modeled. Teachers need structured opportunities to collaborate on decisions, problems, and new ideas within an atmosphere of mutual trust and respect. Even motivated teachers are unlikely to sustain innovations in their own classrooms without the support, trust, and involvement of colleagues. The school as a whole is even less likely to improve without productive interactions and trusting relationships among the teachers.

Trust must permeate the organization for teachers to collaborate and take charge of their own professional development. Administrators help to promote trust by providing support for teachers' efforts, helping them stay focused on student achievement, and giving them leadership and power to carry out change efforts. Teachers need to trust each other as they work together for school improvement. Coaching requires the ultimate trust of receiving feedback and reflecting. Trust can take fear out of the context for learning. Teachers must believe that they can learn new ways to teach and assess. Beliefs are built on trusting people, including their integrity and commitment. Like collaboration, trust must be nurtured step by step and must be reinforced constantly by leaders and teachers at the school and district level.

Personal conversations, well-planned meetings, school newsletters, newspaper articles, site councils, up-to-date Web sites, and a continuous information flow during emergencies build trust with parents and the community. Parents need to know what changes are taking place within the school that will affect their children, and schools need to solicit and consider parents' feedback before implementing major changes. Parents need to trust that teachers and administrators will retool constantly, as do other professionals (doctors, lawyers, and engineers), to keep up with changing times and expanding knowledge. Parents understand that, as professionals, teachers cannot depend on knowledge gained from college two or more decades ago to meet the needs of today's students. Just as doctors don't operate on the knowledge they had when they left medical school thirty years ago, teachers cannot effectively function without updating their skills. Parents must trust that when teachers are involved in professional development, they are developing skills and abilities to meet the learning needs of their students. They should be informed about the relevance of new knowledge in the following areas:

Instructional strategies and how students learn

Uses of technology

Changes in student population and greater diversity—and how teachers will meet these changing needs

New demands on schools to create informed citizens and productive workers

When teachers leave their classrooms for continued learning, parents must trust that teachers' professional growth will ultimately benefit their children.

Collaboration is never easy, and breaking down isolation is difficult. Fullan (1993) discusses the issues of isolation, autonomy, and collaboration. Teachers guard their solitude because it gives them a territory to call their own, provides them with an opportunity to get work done, and shields them from unwanted scrutiny. Although leaders understand a teacher's desire to work alone, one teacher cannot meet the increased academic performance needs of students without reaping the benefits of intellectual support from colleagues who share research, analyze student work together, use technology, develop new curricula, and update their teaching strategies.

Hargreaves and Dawe (1990) cautioned against contrived collegiality, when administrators impose superficial forms of collaboration on a school culture that is still isolationist at heart. Schools need to foster genuine collaboration that stems from committing to shared goals and recognizing the necessity to work together to achieve them. Again, common time to work together is a means of fostering collaboration among teachers when they work as grade-level teams sharing lessons, creating team units, or reading books together and reflecting on their implications for their school. Collaboration is also evident when committee members use consensus building to make decisions on curriculum or school budgets. As mentioned before, two of the most powerful forms of teacher collaboration are involvement in designing and implementing professional development and peer coaching. In the context of their work together, learning skills in such areas as group facilitation, conflict management, and other group-process skills helps develop and sustain teachers. Their collaborative efforts break the norm of isolation found in schools. Different schools approach collaboration development in various ways, but it is important for teachers and the principal to acknowledge the significance of collaborative work as they nurture the relationships that strengthen collaboration.

Collaboration within the school is important; however, collaboration should extend beyond the school to inform teacher practice. Teachers can collaborate at the district level with other teachers who share their concerns and restraints. Through state or national collegial networks, such as the National Writing Project (or other subject matter projects) or the Coalition of Essential Schools (educational philosophies and instructional methods), teachers and principals can share problems and successes that transcend the boundaries of districts or regions. Their involvement provides them with opportunities to develop, implement, and discuss new approaches in a safe and supportive environment. Networks provide members with opportunities to attend conferences, publish articles, and exchange information through discussions, correspondence, electronic forums, newsgroups, and other formats. Teachers can interact with experts and peers at different times by exchanging e-mail, asking questions, sharing experiences, and discussing issues. The community of learners in networks reduces teacher isolation and increases collaboration without regard to location and time.

Incentives and Recognition

Most teachers are intrinsically motivated to keep learning, but how is this motivation sustained for teachers throughout their careers? What incentives or recognition will be meaningful for teachers? Recognition in its various forms acknowledges from within the school and district the valuable work of teachers. Teachers often respond that time and appreciation, as well as professional treatment, are ways to recognize their efforts for continuous professional development. Treating teachers professionally and recognizing their efforts may include providing materials, a dinner, or refreshments at an activity they are sponsoring; providing release time to work with others on a unit of curriculum; or giving formal recognition at a school board meeting. Stipends, supplementary materials related to a training they attended, or equipment, such as computers or software, are incentives for teachers that provide real and visible rewards for their work in professional growth. These incentives recognize that the teacher participated in and is open to new learning. Publicly recognizing teachers' professional development efforts without creating animosity is important.

Time, however, remains the greatest incentive for teachers. Building time for quality professional development within a teacher's workday or year is crucial. Superintendents and principals who commit to recognizing and honoring teachers for their continued learning for school improvement legitimize professional learning in the eyes of teachers, administrators, parents, and communities.

Resources

Teachers need access to adequate as well as enriching resources, such as research, effective practices from inside and outside their schools, assistance by accomplished practitioners as coaches, and experts' creative ideas on subject matter, instructional methods, and school organization. Resources are fundamental to supporting reform efforts and influencing teacher and administrator abilities to implement change (Guskey, 2000). Lack of resources or spreading resources so thin that they have little impact may hinder the implementation of a well-designed professional development plan. Targeting resources where they can have the greatest effect is a strategic way of using limited resources in schools and districts. Without the proper resources, teachers can become disillusioned with the innovations because materials, books, supplies, equipment, software, technology, or facilities are not available to help them implement what they have learned and are ready to apply.

Professional development cannot take place without the proper resources being made available to teachers in the implementation stage. Use of the computer and the links it can make for teachers electronically are barely explored resources for information and assistance. Using electronic forums and e-mail allows teachers with common interests to share information and ideas, but for these to be useful teachers need consistently functioning, up-to-date technology and easy access. Again, nothing is more frustrating for a motivated and passionate teacher trying to implement new strategies than a lack of the proper resources. Leaders must assure teachers that their professional development work is important by providing the necessary resources and support.

PROCESSES FOR PROFESSIONAL DEVELOPMENT

Teachers are interested in the processes or the how's of professional development, so that they have opportunities to acquire and reflect on new knowledge, strategies, and behaviors. Teachers need to think about their own professional development, schoolwide improvement, and the level of impact that professional development processes will have on their own practices. Table 3.2 serves as a guide when considering different types of professional development activities and how they affect a teacher's practice.

Each type of professional development has a purpose and a level of impact, both of which must be weighed in the overall design for school and student improvement. Multiple processes must be used for a sustained effect so that new knowledge and strategies can be applied and evaluated in the teacher's classroom. Balance and infusion of ideas from the outside expertise as well as inside expertise should be used to inform professional practice within the school setting (see Figure 3.3, p. 72). Lieberman and Miller (1999) describe this balance as taking on three organizational forms: direct teaching (workshops), learning in school, and learning out of school. These organizational forms for professional development provide for support and pressure, coupled with multiple entry points that are sensitive to teachers' career stages, and offer many opportunities to grow professionally (Lieberman & Miller, 1999). It is important to understand how professional development activities interact, connect, and build on past experiences and present needs and when outside expertise and research are needed to inform and enhance professional learning within the school.

We hope that the days of disconnected professional development events staged for teacher learning are gone. The coherence of a balanced and infused professional development plan supports the overall school improvement efforts in a systemic way. Educators should view Figure 3.3 in relation to their school's professional development plan. What insights do you gain about balance and infusion in your school's professional learning? What would other teachers within your school say about the balance and infusion of professional development practices?

Using Figure 3.3 as a tool, a school could survey and assess the status of each teacher's professional learning (direct, inside, and outside). These data could be used to inform the schoolwide professional development plan. Too often, assumptions are made about where teachers and administrators need to grow professionally, but there is a failure to assess the current status of learning of individuals within the school. Such an assessment could provide valuable information for professional growth that meets the learning needs rather than prescribing activities that are inappropriate. Also, it could serve as a resource for information about which teachers have expertise or experience with specific curricula, instructional strategies, or assessments that could be shared within the

Table 3.2   Professional Development Processes: Impact and Use

Type	Length	Level of Use	Level of Impact
Onetime workshop	Episodic, onetime	Awareness of new idea or strategy	Little or none Less than 5%
Series of workshops	2–3 days	Awareness, practice	Beginning use Less than 5%
Series of workshops	3–12 months	Awareness, practice Beginning implementation	Implementation Developmental level
Practice, feedback, coaching	Ongoing	Ongoing coaching	Continued use
Job embedded	Daily	Research into practice Observation, reflection	Inquiry into practice
Cycle of inquiry, action research	Ongoing	Research into practice	Study of issue Understanding outcomes
Networks	Periodic	Awareness and sharing, reflection	Reinforces work
Conferences	Periodic	Awareness and sharing	Little or none
Summer institutes	Periodic	Awareness, development, practice, reflection	Little or none

school and district. Tapping the knowledge base of a school's teaching force not only validates teachers' expertise but also provides a rich resource for shared knowledge within a school and district.

PROFESSIONAL DEVELOPMENT PLANS: INDIVIDUAL, TEAM, AND SCHOOLWIDE

Individual Plans

Individual professional development plans link learning to the immediate and real problems faced by teachers. Professional development

Figure 3.3   Professional Development: Balance and Infusion of Learning in
Professional Practice

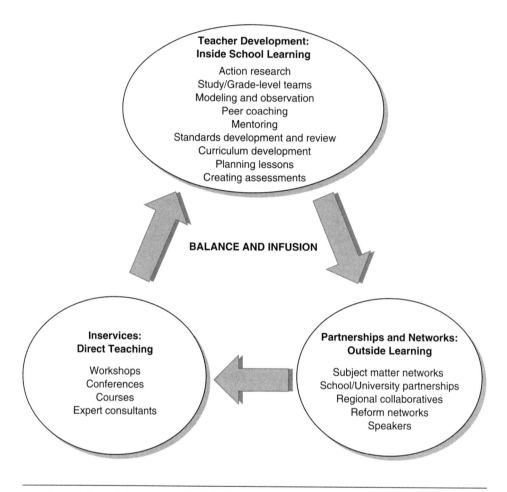

SOURCE: Adapted from research of Lieberman and Miller (1999).

designed by the individual teacher assumes that the most powerful
learning is that which occurs in response to the current needs of a teacher.
It allows for immediate application, experimentation, and adaptation in
the classroom by the teacher (Sparks & Hirsh, 1997). Recognizing and supporting individually guided professional development provides opportunities for principals or superintendents to help each teacher's growth in
unique ways while still supporting overall school improvement goals
(Tracy & Schuttenberg, 1990). The self-directed model is designed to assist
both the individual and the school organization in achieving mutually
agreed-on goals of increased student achievement.

Helping teachers not only design but also be accountable for their own
learning and professional development is critical to the process.

Supporting teachers as they develop individual pathways to learning provides each teacher not only with freedom of choice but also with clear expectations that their efforts must focus on students and help increase student success.

A variety of delivery patterns and clearly laid out growth opportunities has the most potential for satisfying the diverse needs of any school staff while remaining congruent with a larger frame. Professional development choices need to be goal directed and have some common thread that enhances previous experiences while developing new learnings (Lipton & Greenblatt, 1992, p. 24).

Supporting Individual Pathways and Adult Learning

By supporting individual pathways for professional development, the school can model a learning community approach to teacher growth. As teachers design their own professional growth, they model for others life-long learning habits as members of a vibrant school learning community. These individual pathways must honor what we know about adult learning and the implications for professional development (Joyce & Showers, 2002; Little, 1993a; National Staff Development Council, 2001; Speck, 1996):

- Adults will commit to learning when they believe that the objectives are realistic and important for their personal and professional needs. They need to see that what they learn through professional development is relevant and applicable to their day-to-day activities and problems.
- Adults want to be the origin of their own learning and should therefore have some control over the what, who, how, why, when, and where of their learning, as long as it meets the criterion of increasing teacher capacity to affect student achievement.
- Adults will resist activities they see as an attack on their competence. Professional development must be structured to provide support from peers and to reduce the fear of judgment.
- Adult learners need direct, concrete experiences for applying what they have learned to their work.
- Adult learners do not automatically transfer learning into daily practice. Coaching and other kinds of follow-up support are needed so that the learning is sustained.
- Adults need to receive feedback on the results of their efforts. Professional development activities must include opportunities for individuals to practice new skills and receive structured, helpful feedback.
- Adults should participate in small-group activities during the learning process. By providing opportunities to share, reflect, and generalize their learning and experiences, these small groups help

adult learners move from simply understanding the new materials to the desired levels of application, analysis, synthesis, and evaluation.

- Adult learners come to the learning process with self-direction and a wide range of previous experiences, knowledge, interests, and competencies. This diversity must be accommodated in the planning and implementation of professional development.
- Adults enjoy novelty and variety in their learning experiences, and learning opportunities need to reflect these critical attributes of quality professional development.

Individually guided professional development plans should recognize these adult learning needs and provide a means for meeting the diversity of needs, interests, and learning styles of teachers within a school. The school reform efforts focus on individualizing and personalizing learning. What better way to model this for teachers than by promoting and honoring the depth of an individual teacher's own professional development plan? Providing opportunities for teachers to exercise professional judgment about their learning empowers them as professionals to reflect on their practices and needs for improvement. Nothing sends a clearer message than the district's articulation of what is important in professional development. Individualized professional development and school-based changes are mutually supportive. One without the other renders either strategy unattainable. Together, they create a climate to support more effective learning for both students and teachers. Practiced together and balanced, they will transform schools into learning communities.

The design of individual professional development plans cannot be vague. Otherwise, the commitment of individual teachers to carry out their professional development plans lapses into good intentions, and something always forestalls their carrying out the plans. Teachers should analyze their current status as professionals, their classroom needs, the needs of their students, and the data that are available regarding student learning and achievement. Using this analysis as a starting point, teachers can develop the beginning elements of their individualized plans. Planning for professional growth does not consist of teachers' picking a workshop here and there. Individual professional development plans need to be structured with specific goals, which need to be met by specific actions on the part of the teacher. For example, a teacher might select participation in a series of grade-level meetings to examine student-written work to determine the strengths and weaknesses of the writing curriculum. Or if most students are failing estimation on the math exams, it is obvious that the teacher needs to include estimation as part of the curriculum and needs strategies for teaching this concept. Individual teachers may use professional development time to research training for themselves and later to embed appropriate learning and assessment strategies into the curriculum to meet their students' deficiencies. Assuming that raising math scores is a district goal, the principal as well as the teachers will be able to see the alignment of intentions, actions, and district goals and yet still meet individual teacher learning needs and abilities.

As professionals, teachers also need to look deeply into where they are in their career and where they should continue to develop. Individualized professional growth is not haphazard; instead, it is well planned and includes reflection time. Administrators should provide appropriate support for teachers to carry out their individualized plans. Administrators also help by focusing the teacher on the overall school and district goals that the individualized plan will help promote. It is this *balance* that must be kept in focus—between *individualizing* to meet a teacher's learning needs and working *together interdependently* to improve the school and student achievement.

Career stages and developmental needs of teachers are critical pieces in an individual's professional development process. By reviewing where they are in their careers and assessing their developmental needs, teachers will have a better understanding of how to keep themselves professionally current, excited about teaching, and moving toward appropriate goals. Table 3.3 is a tool for teachers to examine their developmental needs based on their career experiences. After reviewing the career stages, principals, too, will have a better understanding of teachers' developmental needs. These needs are very different for teachers in the first, formative years in the classroom versus senior teachers a few years from retirement. This individualized

Table 3.3   Career Stages and Developmental Needs

Career Stage		*Developmental Needs*
Formative years	1–2	Survival Stage: Needs to learn day-to-day operations of classroom and school
Building years	3–5	Building Stage: Develops confidence in work and multifaceted role of teaching
Striving years	5–8	Striving Stage: Seeks to develop professionally and achieve high job satisfaction
Crisis periods	Varies	Teacher burnout and need for renewal
Complacency	Varies	Complacency and low innovation
Career wind down	Varies	High status as a teacher without exerting much effort
Career end	Varies	Retirement

SOURCE: Based on the work of Burden (1982); Burke, Christensen, and Fessler (1984); Christensen, Burke, Fessler, and Hagstrom (1983); Feiman and Floden (1980); Newman, Dornburg, Dubois, and Kranz (1980); and Ponticell and Zepeda (1996).

assessment of where teachers are in their careers honors teachers as professionals and creates the expectation for creative, needs-based individual professional growth plans designed and owned by teachers.

DESIGNING INDIVIDUALIZED PROFESSIONAL DEVELOPMENT

As individual teachers design their personal professional development plans, Figure 3.4 will help focus the effort. The Personal Cycle of Inquiry invites teachers to complete a needs assessment, determine a focus, create a plan, carry out the plan, apply new learning in the classroom, reflect on the application, and evaluate the learning outcomes. The cycle is effective when used to inform teachers of their ongoing needs and plans for continuous growth and application of learning. As each step of the Personal Cycle of Inquiry is accomplished, the teacher's understanding of content and strategies is deepened, and the teacher applies the new learning and reflects on it, including analyzing its effectiveness with students. Too often, the professional development plans of individuals consist of series of activities with little application or reflection as to how the information and strategies will be used in the classroom. With a clear plan of action, teachers can make intelligent and reasoned judgments of appropriate professional development opportunities that will meet their professional development goals in a systematic way. Each of the areas within the Personal Cycle of Inquiry is reviewed by first raising a series of important questions and then discussing the importance of the area to keeping a clear focus for the individualized professional development plan for increasing student achievement.

THE PERSONAL CYCLE OF INQUIRY

Assess Learning Needs

Where am I in my career?

What are my students' needs and achievement levels?

What data have I analyzed?

How am I prepared to meet my students' needs?

What are my school goals and how do they relate to my professional learning needs?

What do I want to learn to improve my students' achievement?

What are the priority areas I need to develop to increase my students' achievement?

Figure 3.4   Personal Cycle of Inquiry

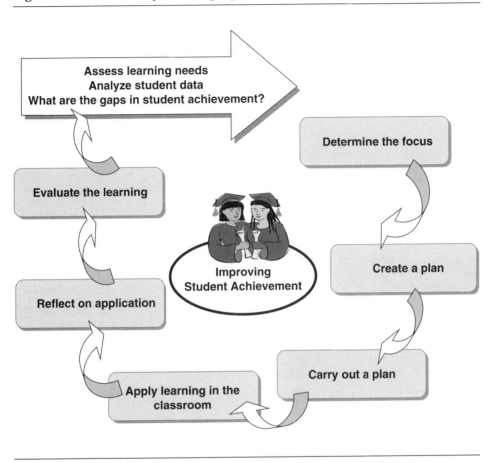

Assess Learning Needs

In using the Personal Cycle of Inquiry (Figure 3.4), teachers must first look at where they are in their professional careers and where they want to grow professionally. Career stages and developmental levels are important factors in the needs assessment process for teachers. The needs assessment process (see "Assess Learning Needs" questions) allows a teacher to identify areas for growth, as related to classroom and student needs as well as overall school goals. Examining student work and achievement data is critical at this point since it provides key indicators of areas where students are not achieving and that teachers need to address. Individual teachers assessing their own students' needs focuses the professional learning that needs to take place. This process helps to prioritize what is important for the teacher to focus on because the vision of what needs to be learned and how it must be demonstrated is very clear. When teachers are empowered to assess their own learning needs and then to determine appropriate avenues for their development, they take ownership of the assessment and planning process.

Determine the Focus

Where will I focus my development?

Who will help me clarify the focus of my work?

Will my focused work help students to achieve?

How will my focus help promote schoolwide and district goals?

How will I know?

Determine the Focus

Developing a clear focus for the professional development plan helps teachers stay centered on their professional growth. Too often, teachers can become distracted by the daily routine of schoolwork and fail to find the time to focus on their own growth needs. By creating a clear focus, teachers can target their efforts in professional development. The focus should emphasize impact on student achievement, which is the heart of every teacher's work.

Create a Plan

What are my plans for carrying out my focused work?

What resources and support do I have to help me?

What connections can I make with others to help develop my plan or our plans?

Create a Plan

Planning allows teachers and administrators to focus the professional development work with a clear process so that it can be carried out. Without a plan, teachers can drift from one focus to another without any validation for their efforts. A plan helps teachers reach a destination and clarifies how to spend their professional development time. The professional development plan becomes a road map for the teacher and allows for focus and depth of understanding to occur.

Carry Out a Plan

How will I determine the professional development opportunities that best meet my needs and plans?

How will I schedule and carry out the professional development plan?

Carry Out a Plan

Professional development activities with a clearly defined plan become an important means of carrying out a teacher's focus. A thoughtful plan, with the specific types of professional development activities laid out, provides a systematic means of reaching the teacher's professional growth goals.

Apply Learning in the Classroom

What are my plans for applying the new learning to my classroom?

What will be different for students as a result of the plan when applied in the classroom?

How can I involve others in helping me plan the integration of these new ideas and concepts with the current curriculum?

How will the new learning affect my students?

Will it address their needs?

Apply Learning in the Classroom

How the teacher applies new learning and insights in the classroom after a professional development seminar on content or strategies is critical. Without application and adjustments to specific classroom settings, teachers will not experience the power and influence of new information. The new learning must fit with identified student learning needs and must be tailored to an individual teacher's classroom situation. Professional development opportunities that plan coaching and feedback can help teachers as they apply new learnings in their classrooms so that the new practice is understood, refined, used, and assessed on a regular basis.

Reflect on Application

How will I reflect on my learning and application of ideas in the classroom?

How will I know that the application of these learnings will improve student learning?

What difference has my professional learning had on my classroom and student learning?

How have I expanded my repertoire as a teacher?

Reflect on Application

Reflection on the application and practice of new learning is important if teachers are to fully understand the effect of a new concept or strategy. After implementing a new practice, a teacher needs additional professional development time to reflect on the success of the implementation and to determine if it met the intended outcomes. Reflective questions can help focus the work: Was the strategy implemented correctly? Were the right resources used? Were the processes clear? How did it align what is written in the curriculum with what was taught and assessed?

Reflection on the new learning and its application in the classroom allows teachers time to see what influence the professional development had on them and their students. Reflections are more effective if shared with colleagues who used the same information or strategies. A variety of implementation experiences will surface. This reflection process allows individual teachers to understand if their situations are unique and to compare experiences with others who have had the same difficulties or successes. Not only does reflection cause the curriculum and teacher behavior to change, but these changes also affect student learning and achievement.

Evaluate the Learning

How will I know that I have met my focus and goals?

How will my new learnings influence my future growth?

Given my current level of professional knowledge, what plans can I now make for additional growth?

Evaluate the Learning

Knowing whether the professional development's focus was appropriate, the follow-up plan was feasible, and the activities were relevant, as well as whether it had the potential to make a difference for students, is important for teachers to assess. Evaluation of how far a teacher has grown is an important part of the individualized professional development process. Evaluation and self-assessment provide new knowledge of what has been learned and of what a teacher needs as a continued or expanded area of focused growth. Too often, an educator experiences professional growth activities but never has follow-through or evaluates whether or not the activities were effective or how they fit into his or her overall plan to gain expertise. Evaluation sets the stage for an ongoing process of professional development and meeting goals. The results of the evaluation process provide information with which teachers can begin to design their next steps in the quest to keep professionally current.

Table 3.4 is provided for teachers to use in developing their own professional development plans. These guiding questions, which summarize the Personal Cycle of Inquiry, help teachers determine their own cycle of inquiry into their teaching practices and to plan their own individualized professional growth. The questions help individual teachers determine needs, prioritize, plan, and evaluate their own learning.

Table 3.4   Guiding Questions: Personal Cycle of Inquiry

Teacher Name: _____   **School Year:** _____
Assess Learning Needs
Where am I in my career?
What are my students' needs and achievement levels?
What data have I analyzed?
How am I prepared to meet my students' needs?
What are my school goals and how do they relate to my professional learning needs?
What do I want to learn to improve my students' achievement?
What are the priority areas I need to develop to increase my students' achievement?

(Continued)

Table 3.4 (Continued)

Determine the Focus

Where will I focus my development?

Who will help me clarify the focus of my work?

Will my focused work help students to achieve?

How will my focus help promote schoolwide and district goals?

How will I know?

Create a Plan

What are my plans for carrying out my focused work?

What resources and support do I have to help me?

What connections can I make with others to help develop my plan or our plans?

Carry Out a Plan

How will I determine the professional development opportunities that best meet my needs and plans?

How will I schedule and carry out the professional development plan?

Apply Learning in the Classroom

What are my plans for applying the new learning to my classroom?

What will be different for students as a result of the plan when applied in the classroom?

How can I involve others in helping me plan the integration of these new ideas and concepts with the current curriculum?

How will the new learning affect my students?

Will it address their needs?

Reflect on Application

How will I reflect on my learning and application of ideas in the classroom?

How will I know that the application of these learnings will improve student learning?

What difference has my professional learning had on my classroom and student learning?

How have I expanded my repertoire as a teacher?

Evaluate the Learning

How will I know that I have met my focus and goals?

How will my new learnings influence my future growth?

Given my current level of professional knowledge, what plans can I now make for additional growth?

THE TEAM AND SCHOOLWIDE CYCLES OF INQUIRY

The concept of a cycle of inquiry can be adapted to use by teams or schoolwide personnel on an issue of importance. The group process of the cycle of inquiry is the same as the individual cycle of inquiry, but a team or schoolwide effort allows shared inquiry into practices (see Figure 3.5). It is based on analysis of student data, determination of teachers' learning needs (team or schoolwide), and then design of professional development strategies to meet the needs and improve student learning.

CONCLUSION

Professional development planners must take teachers' work concerns seriously if they are to have a significant impact on the continued professional learning of teachers. Recognizing the roles and responsibilities, conditions, and processes of professional development from the perspective of teachers' work concerns provides insights into how professional development is envisioned, planned, and carried out for school improvement. Teachers must be given leadership roles and responsibilities (teacher leader, coach, mentor, etc.) that provide them with the opportunities to lead, present, evaluate, and reflect on their professional learning and growth. By addressing teacher work concerns around the conditions of

Figure 3.5   Team or School Cycle of Inquiry

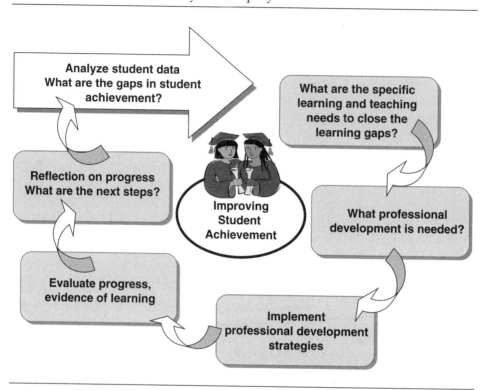

professional development (leadership and policies, time, trust and collaboration, incentives and recognition, resources), a school can plan how to meet the concerns raised by the conditions. To develop a well-designed school professional development plan, teachers and principals should determine together how to respond to teachers' work concerns and learning needs. To incorporate a variety of processes and forms for professional development available to a school, teachers can access both inside and outside sources. When educators recognize the potential of meeting the reality of teacher work concerns through professional development plans (individual, team, and schoolwide), they will have developed a foundation on which to build continuous professional learning for all teachers.

Stop and reflect on these key points and their meaning for student achievement in your school.

KEY POINTS

- Professional development planners must take teachers' work concerns seriously if high-quality professional development is to significantly affect teachers' learning.
- Conditions for professional development (leadership, policies, time, trust and collaboration, incentives and recognition, and resources) must provide a strong foundation on which to build continuous professional learning for teachers.
- Processes and forms of professional development need to be balanced and infused with a variety of opportunities for learning as an individual, through teamwork and on a schoolwide basis. The level of effect and use of various professional development strategies needs to be reviewed in a cost-time/benefit analysis.
- Cycles of inquiry provide the critical processes to analyze student data and teacher learning needs and provide focused professional learning to improve student achievement over time.

4

Designing Your
Own Model

SCENARIO

In the faculty room of a middle school, the planning committee for in-service met to discuss the possibilities. "I think we ought to contact the regional service center to provide facilitation for the two days," began a fifth-grade teacher.

"Why? What would they do?" her colleague questioned.

"They could do a math or science program. I hear they have a way of presenting math concepts that is really a kick."

The second-grade teacher was thoughtfully sipping her tea. "I don't need that right now. What I need is more information about the reading series we just adopted. It has a very different approach to phonics, one I'm not familiar with. I need help." Each of the participants in turn expressed a different idea about the use of professional learning time.

The result was that the meeting was adjourned without making any decisions.

Based on your learning and experience, how would you have guided this discussion? Is it possible to meet the learning needs of teachers and, at the same time, hold the focus on improving student achievement?

+---
ESSENTIAL QUESTION

What professional development designs and tools will be used to focus a learning community on student achievement?

Pause for a moment to reflect on this essential question.
---+

Because educators and researchers are now designating the school as the locus of professional development, we need, more than ever, the knowledge and skills to design effective models of professional development. The models emerge from the need to report results—improved student success. This chapter helps educational leaders responsible for professional development design their own programs for long-term and short-term results. Highlighting some important elements of design to consider when implementing professional development processes provides valuable assistance to principals and teacher leaders. When designers routinely address these elements for acquiring strategies to build a learning community, they create a greater depth to their professional development design. Designating roles and responsibilities in a seminar planning session, for example, carries with it a suggestion for how to avoid creating the in-groups and the out-groups of a school faculty. This chapter examines various design tools to help educators customize their professional development.

POTENT PROFESSIONAL DEVELOPMENT

POTENT is an acronym representing a powerful tool created for designers of a school or district professional development program that includes Purpose and Preparation; Outcomes; Targets and Tools; Energy, Effectiveness, and Evaluation; Numbers, Names, and Needs; and Timelines. The POTENT planning tool can be used to analyze the current program or to plan for significant events within the scope of a multiyear school plan. Using POTENT as a filter for all professional development proposals will challenge school and district staff to realize how high-quality professional development can have a lasting impact on student learning.

Moving from theoretical to the practical, educators know that they must learn new skills to teach all students. They know they need to connect to students and their learning styles, their physical environment, their experiences, their communities, and their readiness. They also need to be more strategic and systemic in their thinking about how to become proficient at reaching each student as they align their outcomes with student achievement. Knowledge about teaching and learning is expanding so rapidly, they need opportunities to stay current with research. Educators need help from researchers' findings and from knowledgeable staff members to implement innovations and refine practices. They need the space and time during the learning phase to reach mastery. If the evaluation of effectiveness warrants it, staff must also have leadership opportunities to share their new skills with others as they become mentors and coaches. These concerns will be addressed as educators begin to design long-term professional development opportunities at the district and site levels.

The acronym POTENT helps leaders determine the elements of a planning process for high-powered or POTENT professional development opportunities. The concept becomes a fractal in that planners can use it to analyze the overall program on a larger scale, yet they can also use the frame for significant opportunities within the scope of their plans. Guided by the POTENT frame provided in this chapter, educators will be practicing systems awareness as they define the relationships, information, and vision for professional development in the internal and external systems of their school (see Figure 4.1, p. 90). In addition, we have included a frame without the significant questions so that designers can write their personal responses using their own issues and data to complete the plan (Figure 4.2, see p. 91).

After the description of each POTENT element in the following sections, we have included a list of questions facilitators should ask when planning professional development opportunities, whether they are in grade-level meetings, department meetings, or with an entire staff. The questions are prompts to make certain the designers have covered all the elements. Be aware that two or more elements may be reflected for each letter of POTENT.

P: Clear Purpose and Adequate Preparation

Aligning professional development with a single purpose (e.g., results in student achievement) ensures that you are pursuing a goal with a focused intent over an extended period of time. The purpose must be visionary with agreement from your district and community that people will care about the results when your purpose is accomplished.

Why is preparing participants to perform the work often neglected? Teachers, for example, are plunged into profound changes in the way they construct curriculum and assessment without understanding why they are feeling resistant or angry. Learning about change and how it will affect their behaviors is critical to the process. Conversely, ignoring the effects of change may needlessly delay the reform efforts from being implemented in an acceptable length of time, if at all. Educators must also be prepared to identify and use high-level communication skills to work together as a powerful, performing team. Bringing about necessary changes in all their complexity is a difficult venture. In fact, without the ability to communicate effectively, formally and informally, on an ongoing basis, new information about teaching and learning will stop with a single teacher and never have the systemic impact of shared knowledge on systemwide student success.

Figure 4.1   How POTENT Is Your Professional Development?

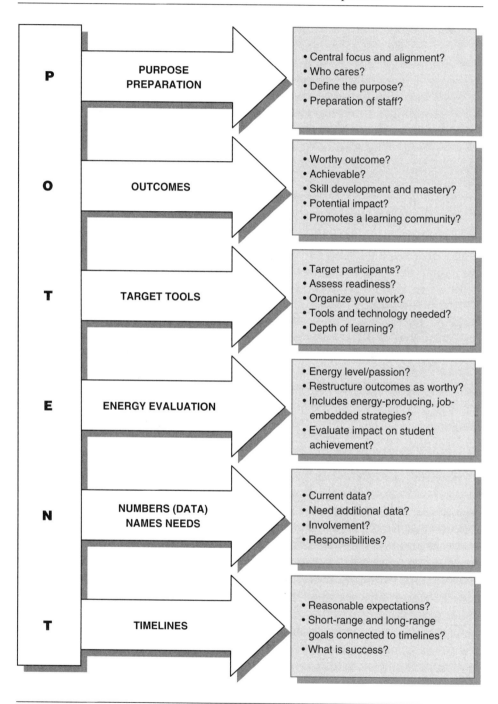

Figure 4.2   How POTENT Is Your Professional Development?

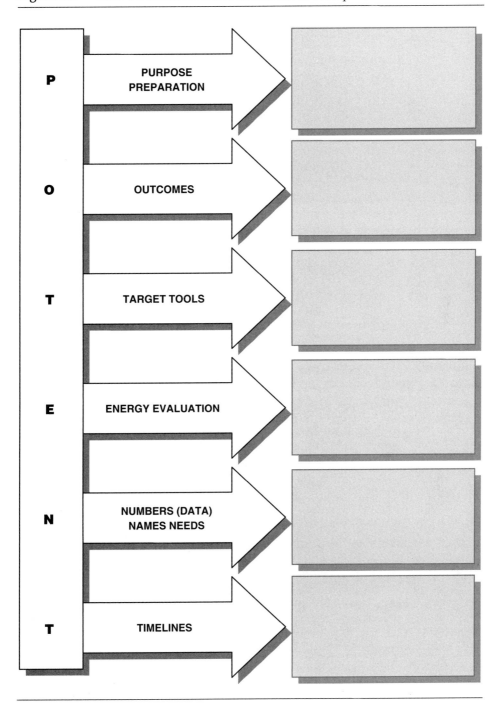

Questions to Consider in Professional Development Planning

1. What is the central focus of your work and how is it aligned with the organization's core purpose?

2. Who cares about this work?

3. How will you clearly define the purpose so that the professional development aligns with your needs?

4. How will you prepare staff with information about how change occurs and how groups of individuals become high-performing teams?

O: Worthy Outcome

The outcomes of your professional development activities, seminars, action research, coaching experiences, or team experiences will vary depending on the topic. It is important to determine before approving the expenditures whether or not the outcomes are worth the cost. The outcomes must be achievable. If the outcome involves learning a new skill, does your outcome also involve opportunities to progress from awareness to mastery to the ability to mentor and coach others? If the outcome involves teaching and learning, does it detail the student achievement that will result? Professional development outcomes should always build on the attributes of a learning community: collaboration, working from data, reflection, inquiry, dialogue, and blameless discussion.

Having clear outcomes is essential to participants because there are no surprises about either what you are planning or the anticipated result of the experience.

Questions to Consider in Professional Development Planning

1. Is your outcome worth the cost?

2. Is it achievable?

3. Does it involve skill development and mastery leading to the ability to mentor and coach others?

4. What is the potential impact on student achievement?

5. Does it promote the attributes of a learning community, including collaboration, working from data, reflection, inquiry, dialogue, and blameless discussion?

T: Target and Tools

When planning, the team needs to establish a target audience as well as a learning target. What level of experience and expertise will the plan target for this work? Experienced teachers become very frustrated if the assumed skill level in the training is out of touch with where they are. Experienced teachers may not need the same depth of involvement to implement new strategies. Conversely, beginning teachers need a safe place to say, "I have no idea about how this will work in a classroom or how to prepare the students." They may not need experienced teachers giving explicit directions. They do need a thoughtful inquiry process that lets them discover and take risks. Professional development planners should take the time to consider these needs.

The learning target must be equally specific. Expanding teachers' knowledge of content and repertoire of teaching and assessment strategies is especially important in teaching to the standards. Teachers using interactive learning to teach specific standards, for example, become proficient in planning not only the learning opportunity but also the assessment so that students are learning, doing, and demonstrating proficiency.

What tools will be needed to do the work? Facilitators can explore tools as configurations for activities, such as large-group or small-group facilitation, or tools may be strategies of facilitation, such as using physical movement as a stimulus to evoke deeper thinking. Tools may also be frames, graphics, computer displays, online case studies, videos, or Web sites that help with researching a topic. Many tools are available to teacher leaders and professional staff developers to deepen the learning: facilitated seminars, coaching, feedback loops, action research, and follow-up in your plan. When planning, it is helpful to broaden the selection of strategies by staying current with the tools of the profession through the National Staff Development Council and through the state affiliates.

Questions to Consider in Professional Development Planning

1. Who are the target participants?

2. How will their readiness be assessed?

3. How will content and strategies be aligned to purpose and outcomes?

4. Are the content and strategies aligned with state and district standards and assessments?

5. What other tools do you need?

6. Will you add depth to the learning by including facilitated seminars, coaching, feedback loops, action research, and follow-up in your plan?

E: Energy, Effectiveness, and Evaluation

Earlier we addressed the need for high energy by team leaders and facilitators for professional development opportunities. If participants don't have some passion for the results of their professional development experience, they need to negotiate with their colleagues about what will increase the overall level of energy. If everyone has low energy for the proposal and tasks, the program may not receive the attention it deserves. Because the needs of teachers are so great for high-quality support, a low-energy project may appropriately be put on hold and replaced with one that meets more urgent needs of the staff.

Effectiveness refers to looking at three levels of impact of professional development. First, consider the potential impact on student achievement. Second, professional development should impact all teachers' accumulation of effective skills and strategies. Third, job-embedded components will ensure the influence on the real work of teachers. Energy tends to increase when the concepts affect student work directly through job-embedded strategies. What is it that teachers will be doing differently in the classroom?

Using a cycle of inquiry (see Chapter 3) and assessing the outcomes give teachers another window to the world of student success and how to achieve it. Fourth, the process should affect other teachers in the system. The professional development plan the leaders are creating should lessen the isolation of teachers and lead to new roles and responsibilities for them within the school organization. One teacher's excellence does not make an effective school, and single schools, although they may be individually effective, do not make an effective district. It is a discipline for individuals to be aware of a school's direction and the impact it will have on the district, but one must regularly assess the bigger picture if education is to serve all students and improve in the eyes of the public.

The evaluation design is of critical importance for looking at what works and what does not work. Teachers in the past have tried various strategies to improve performance but have not held themselves accountable for the effect of the new strategies by looking for results in student work. A solid evaluation instrument helps determine if the strategy needs to be continued, refined, discarded, or replaced with more effective ways of accomplishing the goal. In addition, an evaluation instrument will assess how the implementation has affected teachers' repertoire of effective skills and strategies.

Questions to Consider in Professional Development Planning

1. What energy or passion do you have for pursuing and sustaining the outcomes?

2. How can you negotiate the outcomes so that they are worth your energy and passion?

3. Have you used job-embedded strategies to increase the energy of application and discovery?

4. What processes are in place to evaluate the impact of the work on student achievement?

5. What processes are in place to evaluate the impact on teachers' repertoire of effective skills and strategies?

6. Will the professional development evaluation lead to significant new roles and responsibilities for teachers within the school and district?

N: Numbers and Needs

Should schools embark on professional development plans without data that prove the need? Because teachers are consumed by their daily responsibilities, they must know that what they will accomplish through professional development is important and necessary. Leaders should consider current and projected needs that are substantiated from analyzing data. For example, as a result of examining the data, if students need to learn estimation because their performance in this math area is very low compared with other students of a comparable grade level, you have a valid incentive for professional collaboration on new strategies needed to increase student achievement. The need is urgent and must be weighed against a plan for teachers to be involved in other, less timely activities or processes.

Planners should also be clear about resources—human, financial, or material—in building a professional development plan. Frequently, schools will need particular staff members or parents to participate in designated professional development activities because of their roles in the school. Department chairs or lead teachers may be asked to attend district-level seminars so that they can facilitate the key learnings with their colleagues. If participants are expected to relay important information from the sessions, the facilitator should include in the seminar plans the staff member who will take responsibility for designing the facilitated informational sessions and when they will occur.

Too often we underestimate the time that it takes to implement new strategies and assess their effectiveness, and planners may forget to budget for coaching and substitute costs or dollars needed for materials. In designing a professional development plan, leaders will undoubtedly be asked to prepare a budget for specific components. Be aware that educators can no longer limit the cost of training new skills or strategies to a few facilitated seminars. They can easily attach dollar figures to these initial costs, but the equation must be reconfigured to consider the total investment of human and financial resources in sustained professional skill building.

Understanding the dollar figures when initiating professional growth opportunities may help planners remember to align the purpose of student achievement with worthy outcomes before investing in a design. That brings up another critical point. Investing in a single professional development strategy without understanding its place in the long-term design is foolish because doing so will undoubtedly lead to wasted resources.

Assume that a team of teachers is responding to student failure of particular standards. The teachers search for new knowledge about approaches and strategies to teach the materials and enhance learning. They are also looking for timely assessments that will more accurately reflect a student's progress. The long-term design is successful student performance of the standards. Their short-term objectives are clearly aligned with the goals.

Materials needed for professional development sessions are also important considerations. Hastily duplicated articles or information downloaded from the Internet to a faulty printer may lead to poor quality materials for use by participants. Team leaders, facilitators, and teachers show respect for each other and the time invested in participating by securing the best, most readable materials at their disposal. Teachers who are facilitating sessions supported with material budgets must have access to quality printing.

Being current is another concern in a design. How timely are the handouts and supplementary materials? Like outdated textbooks, outdated seminar materials may mislead participants when more recent research could help them with their concerns. Rapid changes so typical of other professional fields are happening in education, too. The need for today's educators to have newer, more effective materials and strategies for working with today's diversified youth cannot be ignored.

As students and teachers become more demanding, schools and districts will be expected to provide more resources for professional development than ever before. When a district invests in its staff and the community by having quality materials for professional learning aligned with the purpose, the rewards will be higher student performance.

Questions to Consider in Professional Development Planning

1. What data do you have to support your design?

2. What data will you collect on an ongoing basis?

3. Who will be involved and how will they communicate to others?

4. What are their responsibilities for implementation?

5. What human, fiscal, and material resources do you need?

6. How will you budget for long-term implementation of skills and strategies?

7. How will you ensure the quality, readability, and timeliness of materials?

T: Timelines

When educators create professional development opportunities that span two to three years, they must also remain flexible. Planning for only one year is not recommended unless leaders are very much in touch with the direction of the district, and the direction has not changed. A reasonable timeline for cohesive efforts is an important consideration in professional development and one that facilitators and teacher leaders should make very clear at the beginning to avoid misguided expectations on the part of both participants and supervisors. At the same time, everyone understands that other timelines will emerge from doing the work. As each timeline and benchmark is met, everyone has a need to know what success looks like. Without a clear picture of success, efforts can stray from the focus, lacking accountability for results.

Questions to Consider in Professional Development Planning

1. What results can reasonably be expected in one month, one year, or three years?

2. What are the short-range and long-range goals connected to the timelines?

3. What does success look like?

Twenty-first-century participants are far more sophisticated than their counterparts a decade ago. Educators are bombarded with involved graphic representations on television. Colorful animation proliferates on their computer screens. They have the opportunity to request the most recent information and have responses by e-mail within a few hours. Teachers need the most current information a professional development design can produce to help with one of the most difficult jobs in our society: educating today's youth. When planners and facilitators use POTENT as a frame for planning professional development, they are assuring themselves and the people working with them that they are preparing teachers in the best, most effective, professionally executed design they can create.

Design Elements to Consider When Implementing POTENT

The intensive labor of professional development planning and design is seldom visible to participants. Designers must deal with teaching and learning challenges, adult learning strategies, standards and assessment issues, and teacher work concerns. At the same time, they cannot ignore superintendent directives and board policies. In Figure 4.3, we identify professional development issues that control the design of effective programs.

Figure 4.3   Issues That Influence the Design of Effective Professional Learning

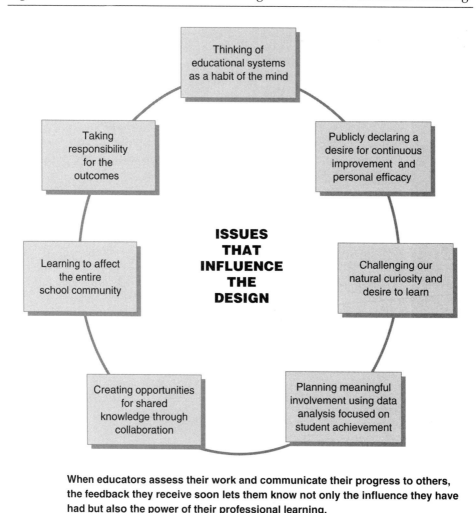

When educators assess their work and communicate their progress to others, the feedback they receive soon lets them know not only the influence they have had but also the power of their professional learning.

If staff members are experiencing programs that seem to be lacking depth, it will be helpful for them to explore these issues.

Thinking of Systems as a Habit of the Mind

As leaders analyze their schools and collaborate with their school communities to initiate change, they are seeking pathways to affect the system. Through understanding how systems work, they learn to look for patterns, processes, and structures that have influenced learning in the past and will shape learning in the future. Leaders may falter in their attempts to change what is currently happening. For example, why did the results stay the same although they changed one aspect of teaching by adopting a new textbook? With no intervention, however, the learning system of teaching strategies, curriculum, environment, and possibly a culture of isolation stayed the same. With more schools on a standards-based system, leaders are supporting standards and assessment as the basis for all curricula. In fact, standards and assessment of the standards form the basis for most decisions in the school affecting teaching and learning, the school environment, and the culture. Changing whole systems is not a series of tasks; it is a commitment to an entirely new way of thinking and acting. When an entire staff decides to change a school to focus on student achievement based on successfully meeting the standards, information about students and student achievement permeate the system. The changes they intend to accomplish are based on their data, and each person has a clear vision about the purpose and direction of the school. Staff members form relationships and networks within and outside of the school with the purpose in mind. The interaction of the relationships, information, and self-referencing based on their clear vision will enable them to sustain their focus and accomplish their purpose.

One of the most challenging exercises is to look personally, then collectively, at how the professional development is impeding or propelling student progress at the site. Because schools are parts of larger systems they cannot be isolated from the larger systems. Every member of the school community has a role in ensuring student success. When individuals acknowledge that they do not live or teach in isolation but that they are vital practitioners within larger systems having continuous interactions affecting students, they are using a very healthy habit of the mind to assess the challenges.

> How can we develop a systemwide professional development design so that we do not become isolated in our thinking or our learning?

Publicly Declaring a Desire for Continuous Improvement and Personal Efficacy

Ask a student which teachers and administrators are no longer learning. Students can tell us very quickly how intellectually alive their teachers are and whether or not they are seeking to improve their teaching. Successful educators seeking a personal efficacy are involved in learning new content, skills, and strategies as models in a learning community. In fact, many educators believe that they already know how to manage and teach, if the students would just do the learning. The holistic way of looking at teaching and learning is that we will never know all there is to know about the educational processes. Strategies for learning and learning together, therefore, have to be a part of what educators, students, parents, and members of a dynamic community do (Barth, 1990).

> What guarantees must be built into our professional development design so that we model learning at all levels?

Challenging Our Natural Curiosity and Desire to Learn

How does the brain function? Educators need to be attentive to brain research when planning professional development in the schools. While the research continues to produce conflicting reports about our neurons and synapses, conclusions about the human traits of natural curiosity and a continuous ability to learn are evident in educational literature. Rockefeller University's McEwen says, "The most important thing is to realize that the brain is growing and changing all the time. It feeds on stimulation and it is never too late to feed it" (Kotulak, 1996, p. 11). One of the primary assailants on neurons is the suppression of curiosity, of the desire to learn. A failure is that educators work very hard to stimulate the brains of students and forget that the brains of adults also need stimulation. Ideas will easily emerge from an exploratory environment. Adults need to be challenged to exert their natural curiosity about teaching and learning.

> What professional development strategies will stimulate curiosity and challenge the desire to learn?

Planning Meaningful Involvement Using Data Analysis Focused on Student Achievement

Humans want some control over what happens to them in the workplace, and this control is a boon to their mental health. Brain researcher Pierce Howard references people who are allowed to take a direct planning and decision-making role in their lives. In summary, they live longer, are sick less, are happier, are more alert, and have less of the stress hormone cortisol (Howard, 1994, p. 64). Teachers want and need to be part of designing, planning, implementing, reviewing, evaluating, and reconfiguring professional development. Aligning these processes to improve student achievement based on their analysis of student data enables teachers to be a part of each student's success.

> How can a professional development design give decision-making powers to staffs while aligning with the vision of student achievement?

Creating Opportunities for Shared Knowledge Through Collaboration

Teachers in a learning community experience the power of shared knowledge. To make responsible decisions, workers in any organization must have a steady flow of information about their work (Wheatley, 1994). They need multiple, multilevel opportunities to build their knowledge base. Teachers who examine content standards together and decide how the standards will be assessed have a basis for building shared knowledge as they create curricula. They decide what skills and strategies will be employed to improve the performance of students and how to collect the results. There is a professional power that comes from having expanded knowledge about how to enable students to be more successful.

How can a professional development design ensure the flow of information to all staff members through continuous opportunities to collaborate?

Learning to Affect the Entire School Community

Sharing and acting on new knowledge about teaching and learning that results in the success of students will in some way flow into every aspect of the larger systems. When a school staff gains the reputation of being in the forefront of learning, the district and other schools, as well as the local school community, benefit. It is from the larger system that teachers need support for their work. Although new knowledge and new strategies don't spread with the same rapidity as bad news or scandal, when educators change their ways of working with colleagues and students, the ripples in the system become supportive waves. Appropriate planning for professional development is one way of determining what educators will do to energize the system and how they will do it. When they assess their work and communicate their progress to others, the feedback they receive soon lets them know not only the influence they have had but also the power of their professional learning.

How can staffs plan professional development so that feedback from their school communities informs their work about how they are affecting the system?

Taking Responsibility for the Outcomes

It wasn't that long ago that a professional development day was considered an ideal time to grade papers and plan one's personal calendar. Today the emphasis is on relevant learning that will affect student achievement in the classroom. Teachers are more involved in the planning of professional development and are able to articulate the outcomes from investing their time in the training and follow-through. The next step is taking responsibility for the outcomes as everyone assesses the influence on student learning.

Design Considerations

When Linda Darling-Hammond (1997) studied successful schools, she identified at least five structures in these schools that supported decentralized information and shared knowledge.

Team planning and teaching allow teachers to share knowledge with one another.

Cross-group structures are used for planning, communication, and decision making.

Professional development is built into the schedule and tied to ongoing homegrown innovations so that teachers learn by doing as they collectively construct new practices.

The schools continually share rich information about students, families, and classroom work through vehicles like narrative report cards, student and teacher portfolios, class and school newsletters, and widely distributed meeting notes. Information about what teachers are doing and how it is working is available everywhere throughout the school.

Highly visible shared exhibitions of student work make it clear what each school values and how students are progressing. Aggregated data about student performance are also regularly available and discussed. (pp. 167–168)

Given the work of Darling-Hammond, how will these structures inform your design?

TOOLS FOR IMPLEMENTATION OF A PROFESSIONAL DEVELOPMENT DESIGN

As teacher leaders respond to the questions outlined in POTENT, they will be searching for additional tools to accelerate implementation. This is the essence of professional development—to think more deeply about how to change old patterns, structures, and processes of teaching and learning for the teacher to help students be more successful. The following tools will assist in your design plan.

Layering the Work

Layering the work is a tool that can be used to explain the alignment of student performance, teacher practice, and professional development. One can look at the educational system in three layers (see Figure 4.4) so that assembled at one time they give an overview of the complicated challenges to be addressed by educators. Layer 1 is student work, with the educational life of a student at the center. Think of what the student is

Figure 4.4   Layering the Work of Implementing a Standards-Based System:
The Work of Students Resonates Throughout the System

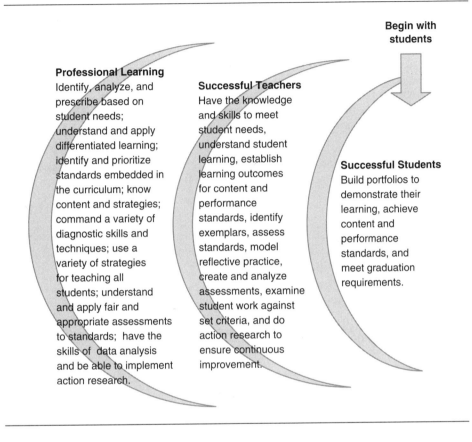

required to accomplish in the public schools. Layer 2 is the work of the teacher. If student success is the focus, each educator will be committed to help each student meet standards. Layer 3 is a plan for professional learning, the key to teachers' continuous capacity to do the work.

Layer 1: Student Work

After nearly two decades in a school system, any senior in a comprehensive high school could complete the information for the graduation requirements in Layer 1. Students must successfully meet district standards for their grade level or subject area. In some schools, they build portfolios of their work connected to content and performance standards. Meeting content standards means that students have learned the subject to a level of competency required by the district and are able to demonstrate their performance through classroom assignments, teacher assessments, performance tasks, and standardized measurements. The student is not expected to complete the work unassisted or unsupported. If the student is having difficulty, the professional team agrees to analyze the student's data and determine which strategies will help him or her achieve the standards.

Layer 2: Teacher Work

As with many professionals, a teacher's work is as complex and intricate as the brain of each recipient. Successful teachers understand and recognize students' needs and goals. With all the recent research on how the brain functions, teachers must have the knowledge of how students learn, which leads directly into teacher work. Designing backward from the standards is a very different way for teachers to think about learning. Teachers assess learning by establishing what the students must know to demonstrate proficiency in meeting the standards. They are not thinking about which activities they will facilitate. They are thinking about what students need to learn and do and how they as teachers can prepare their students to reach the required level of proficiency. Teachers sort through data to determine which assessments will help the students.

It is an unprecedented time for teachers who complained in the past that not enough emphasis was placed on a daily commitment to learning. Analyzing student work with colleagues to establish exemplars of performance helps teachers maintain consistency in answering the question "What level of competency must a student reach to say that he or she has met the standard?" Throughout their classes, teachers model reflective practice as they build life skills in collaboration, problem analysis, problem solving, creative thinking, and technology applications.

The California Standards for the Teaching Profession (California Commission on the Teaching Profession, 1997) begins with "Standards for Engaging and Supporting All Students in Learning" and emphasizes the importance of the classroom.

- Teachers build on students' prior knowledge, life experience, and interests to achieve learning goals for all students.
- Teachers use a variety of instructional strategies and resources that respond to students' diverse needs.
- Teachers facilitate challenging learning experiences for all students in environments that promote autonomy, interaction, and choice.
- Teachers actively engage all students in problem solving and critical thinking within and across subject matter areas.
- Concepts and skills are taught in ways that encourage students to apply them in real-life contexts that make subject matter meaningful.
- Teachers assist all students to become self-directed learners who are able to demonstrate, articulate, and evaluate what they learn. (p. 8)

Layer 3: Professional Learning

Because the work of the teacher is so intense, Layer 3 explores what role teachers play in determining the knowledge, skills, and strategies required to ensure the opportunity for student success. In the content area of reading, for example, effective teachers know how to assess and prescribe to move each student forward at his or her own rate. No teacher can be expected to complete all of the learning tasks relevant to each student in isolation, however. Collaboration and, consequently, the time to collaborate are essential to the professional development process.

If we assume a basic human need to be successful in what we do, all teachers require continuous professional development so that they become even more knowledgeable and more skillful. One fallacy is to believe and act on the belief that professional development prescribed for one instructor is the best for every teacher. Districts must guard against embracing a model that had its roots in an attitude about the basic incompetence of teachers who had to be forced to improve. Even new information will be received and processed at different levels depending on the experiences of the educators. As the public becomes more demanding about specialized programs for students, teachers will become more demanding about their own needs for specialized knowledge. In fact, every member of the school community should be enlisted to support the very demanding work of teachers to improve student achievement.

FRAMES AS VISUAL ORGANIZERS

Using visual tools, such as organizing frames, enhances the learning of participants. In this very visual society, using media and organizers to connect to the learning should be as natural to professional development planners as ordering water and juice in a work session to refresh the bodies and brains of participants.

Frames such as the Personal Cycle of Inquiry discussed in Chapter 3 are visual organizers of our work. They lead participants to deeper discussions because they document progress as they provoke conversation. New realities can be reported to a staff using frames, or they can be helpful in meetings to inform the entire school community. Living the inquiry cycle focuses teams on specific content and teaching strategies to improve student achievement of the standards. It prepares participants for using action research as a basis for ongoing inquiry into the success and achievement of students. The cycle is a basic tool that should be practiced continuously throughout the year.

Generally, frames are graphic or written representations of important components to consider when working on a specific topic. They bring specificity about the work, such as the two column T-chart designating, for example, where we have been and where we are going, or a gap analysis

Figure 4.5   Frames as Visual Organizers of Our Work

Data	Current State ⟶	Desired State ⟶	Assumptions
Thirty-one percent of students are unable to meet grade-level standards on expository writing.	Curriculum for the grade level has not been revised to align with the standards.	Schoolwide, revised curriculum will align with the standards.	When learning focuses on the standards, students will improve their achievement.
Survey shows that parents are unaware of the standards as a measure of student achievement.	Informational attempts to familiarize parents with the standards have been unsuccessful.	All parents will be familiar with and supportive of the standards.	Raising the stakes for students by involving their parents will lead to greater student success.

Frames encourage the staff to focus on the work.

Data Sorted	Teacher Teams	Selected Standards	Action
Data is available for classes of individual teachers.	Teams analyze data to determine which standards and subsections are involved.	The team determines which standards will be the focus for curriculum revision with accompanying teaching materials, strategies, and assessments.	The team begins the Personal Cycle of Inquiry.

following examination of data using current state and desired state followed by articulated assumptions as in Figure 4.5.

Use Frames to Translate Theory Into Practice

Brain research indicates that people who interact with content make it their own, but many group discussions are not focused and, therefore, are not very useful. Frames enable participants to shift from the theoretical to a focused connection with the topic. In past models of professional training on writing curriculum, for example, teachers heard presentations of new writing strategies and then were left on their own to develop related curriculum: "Here are materials or strategies you could use in your classroom." Some teachers tried working with the new information, and some put it aside. In frustration, teachers began to demand make-and-take training so that they could have more immediate application of a concept. Focusing on these short-term innovations, however, did little to improve instruction.

Working collaboratively, teachers use organizers of information as a guide and a means for sharing a process. When teachers write curricula, for example, they follow guides for articulating the outcome and determining the innovations. Because frames reveal the thinking behind the proposed curricular revisions, teachers are able to question each other as they uncover the intent behind the words. As one teacher receives feedback on his or her implementation strategies, other teachers are able to learn a variety of successful strategies for teaching the same content. Conversations lead to a revised curriculum without belaboring every point because teachers are working collaboratively from the same guides and are able to trace the steps of each other's work.

For example, an elementary staff requested a seminar on marine biology from a group specializing in life sciences. In theory, the hands-on experience would enable students to become more deeply involved in their learning. The life science group gave the staff a frame for examining how the activities could fit into the bigger picture of a standards-based curriculum while causing learning to be more interactive for students. The goal was for students to attain a higher level of achievement on related standards.

As part of the seminar, the group's facilitators took volunteers to nearby tide pools along the northern coast of the Pacific Ocean to explore the habitat of varieties of animal life. The teachers were both fascinated and energized. When they returned, they were determined to see how they could incorporate what they had just experienced into their science units. Following their process frame, they first analyzed their grade-level standards and confirmed how the standards would be assessed. Once they came to a consensus on the priorities for learning, they were able to determine if using tide pools would help students achieve the standards. Now that the teachers had affirmed their direction, they could return to the training room for the next steps on writing meaningful curricula. If other grade levels become involved, the teachers who have worked through the process could act as coaches to their peers.

Figure 4.6 (p. 108) examines the life science project. Figure 4.7 (p. 109) encourages the reader to test a recent addition to the curriculum to determine if the events are aligned with the standards.

Figure 4.6   Frames Focus the Work: Determining the Learning Value of New Processes

Life Science Presentation

Which *standards* will be met by the life science project?

What is your *assessment* of the learning? How will you know the student has been successful in achieving these life science standards?

Does the life science activity help students *meet the standards*? Is the science learning meaningful and relevant to the standards? Is the learning enriched by the life science experience?

Which Standards Will Be Met by This Project?

Is time built in for *teacher learning* and preparation before the field trip? Are materials accessible? Are resources available to take advantage of the trip to the tide pools?

If the school decides to adopt the life science program, will other grade levels be involved? Is *peer coaching* an option?

Not especially interested in adopting an entirely different curriculum, the staff welcomed the facilitators' organizer that walked teachers through a process for relating their life science unit to specific standards and performance assessments. Having already decided how they would assess whether or not their students met the standards, the teachers were ready to revise their units of study with appropriate benchmarks. Although the process took several weeks, they met on a regular time schedule to share their progress. During the process they created another frame for sharing alternative strategies for students who were having difficulty with the

Figure 4.7   Frames Focus the Work: Determining the Learning Value of New Processes

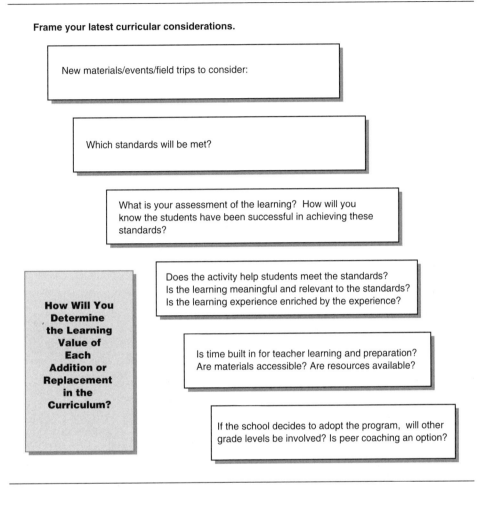

Frame your latest curricular considerations.

New materials/events/field trips to consider:

Which standards will be met?

What is your assessment of the learning? How will you know the students have been successful in achieving these standards?

Does the activity help students meet the standards?
Is the learning meaningful and relevant to the standards?
Is the learning experience enriched by the experience?

Is time built in for teacher learning and preparation?
Are materials accessible? Are resources available?

If the school decides to adopt the program, will other grade levels be involved? Is peer coaching an option?

How Will You Determine the Learning Value of Each Addition or Replacement in the Curriculum?

standards. As teachers field-tested their units, they prepared to share student work using other frames they had devised for collecting and analyzing the results as well as for planning next steps.

Use Frames to Focus Energies

When participants are completing team efforts over an extended period of time, they face the need to continuously refocus the energies of the group. With knowledge of brain research, educators understand that the brain is a parallel processor and that many concerns, pictures, ideas, and floating thoughts occupy one's mental day. The challenge is how to continuously refocus teams to maximize the time they invest in collaboration. Used appropriately, the frame is a discipline, symbolic of "getting to work." When frames as organizers are distributed or posted, the larger group can move quickly to determine the outcomes, and, guided by the frames, the team members work through the processes, recording as they go. Teams will sustain their focus for several hours at a time, energized by their very visible progress as recorded on wall organizers.

Use Frames to Make Visible a Group's Memory and Lead Participants to Deeper Discussions

Wall charts are frames for group memory. Printed or drawn, they should be from six to eight feet long with smaller copies in participant packets. As our society becomes more visually dependent, large and small groups benefit from seeing their progress and the components of their work on a wall chart (see Figure 4.8). Facilitators are free to move the process along as recorders translate the group's thinking to the chart. Team leaders will know the group is correctly processing frames when a participant says, "That's not exactly what I said" and walks to the chart to correct the record or "Let's rethink that action" or "Let's record what each of us said we would do." The frame is not simply a recording but documentation of the group's interactive decision making. When groups individually sign their wall chart, they take ownership from their public declaration for the outcomes. Follow-up for the day's meeting should include e-mail to teachers summarizing the day's work.

A wall frame is most useful when it chronicles a group's work and then is posted where it can be seen over several days so that participants have an opportunity to reflect on their direction. These frames inform others and provoke conversation outside the team that created it. As educators develop their system awareness, they will know the importance of getting feedback from others for reshaping the work. Another reason for using six- to eight-foot charts is that when either works in progress or completed frames are shared in a school and district, the conversations that took place in other groups are reported accurately.

"No surprises" is the rule in human relations. If a school, for example, is identified by the state as low performing, the staff needs to understand, first, what that means and, second, what steps they will take to correct the inequities. With several teams working on various aspects of a problem, the information flow can easily be blocked. With the use of frames, the communication lines are opened. The teams analyze the problem based on data and then post their charts. The faculty convenes to look at the charts reflecting investigations by the various teams before they take steps to address the concern. In data-driven decision-making processes, the data and problem analyses are shared and action plans agreed on as part of a

Figure 4.8 Wall Charts Make a Team's Planning Visible

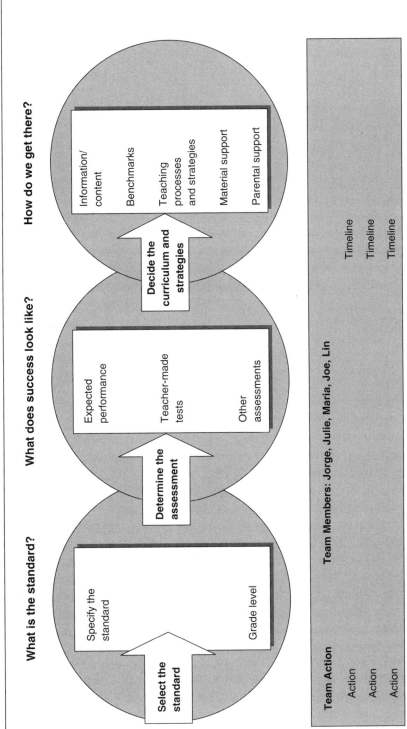

What is the standard?

What does success look like?

How do we get there?

Specify the standard

Grade level

Select the standard

Determine the assessment

Expected performance

Teacher-made tests

Other assessments

Decide the curriculum and strategies

Information/content

Benchmarks

Teaching processes and strategies

Material support

Parental support

Team Members: Jorge, Julie, Maria, Joe, Lin

Team Action

Action   Timeline

Action   Timeline

Action   Timeline

cohesive plan. In comprehensive high schools, large middle schools, or large elementary schools with modular classrooms, it is very important to share these realities in a systematic, highly visible format.

For example, an elementary school was having difficulty with the term *low performing*. When various teams analyzed the problems of low-performing students using a format of "data," "current problem," and "desired state" along with suggested "next steps," they realized that they did not all agree on what the problems were, nor did they agree on what was a desired state for all students. Retracing the problem to their values, beliefs, and assumptions about their students' abilities made arriving at conclusions about how to improve learning more complicated. Easy answers, including blaming others, that were suggested at the beginning of the meeting were replaced by more thoughtful ways to approach the low-performance problem and possible steps they could take that would have lasting effects.

Use Frames to Inform the Entire School Community

Frequently, wall frames reflecting professional learning and agreed-on directions are taken to the community to form a backdrop, while the principal or other key leaders explain the process. A faculty may ask a leadership team, for example, to research how class schedules influence student learning. The result may be a major decision to revise class schedules that has implications for the entire school community. Wall frames can show how the leadership team's work included community involvement. When a community has been asked for feedback, it is important for them to see how the feedback was used. Bringing proposed actions back to a group using a graphic format is a way of closing the communication loop from being informed and giving feedback to seeing what happened as a result. It is a reasonable way to inform the school community in that it also publicly honors the time people invested in providing feedback. Because the district values community involvement, community members will be more willing to participate in the future.

PEOPLE CONNECTIONS IN PROFESSIONAL SETTINGS

Connections are the way we link people engaged in their own professional learning. How to connect people involved in various professional development constructs should be a part of the overall plan. First, think about level of experience. In grade-level teams, experienced teachers could be linked with new teachers. Since beginning teachers may be more familiar with recent research through their classes at the university, they may provide a fresh perspective to established ways of thinking. More experienced teachers provide the reality of years of working with students. Forming these connections helps teachers to view units of study from different perspectives. These various perspectives are essential for informing and changing a system.

Second, schools are becoming more aware of how connections within and among a diverse faculty provide a distinctive richness to the curriculum. In preparing a unit on ancient cultures, for example, teachers discovered that one faculty member had been raised with traditions that were thousands of years old. Her father was a Buddhist monk in Japan. Her personal knowledge greatly enriched students' ability to contrast cultures, which was embedded in the history standard. Without the team's collaboration, only the teacher's own class would have benefited from her vast knowledge and collection of artifacts. Because the faculty was working in cross-grade-level teams, teachers were able to deepen their own knowledge of the curriculum and make it richer for students.

Third, ensuring that faculty members make connections with other teachers they don't normally see during the school day is a way of developing professional relationships that will perpetuate a school's culture of openness to ideas. When an entire district is focused on student achievement, districtwide, teacher-led discussions of student performance and curricular strategies become a necessary part of a strategic plan.

A MATRIX TO SUMMARIZE DATA

A matrix is a helpful tool for principals who want to see their faculty's involvement at a glance, as in Figure 4.9. Across the top, the principal lists the many teams and committees in the school and district. Down the left side of the matrix is a list of faculty members. The principal assesses each teacher's investment of time in collaborative efforts by moving across the table of possible involvement, recording yes or no for each activity. As a principal reads the matrix, it is easy to see which committees each teacher has chosen or was assigned to. Principals who take the time to keep the list current quickly see faculty members who are involved and those who haven't made any connections. Although new teachers especially need to be protected while they are learning their skills, experienced teachers need to be system-wise. Teachers experiencing meaningful collaboration with educators from other schools can reduce their feelings of anxiety and competition when test scores are published. The negative feelings are replaced by the knowledge that schools are helping each other. Teachers feel supported when they are involved in meaningful, collaborative efforts on a larger scale.

Traditional ways of connecting people (large and small groups within a particular setting or training, grade-level teams, content area teams, cross-grade-level teams, action research teams, schoolwide teams focused on a

Figure 4.9   Matrix of Teacher Involvement

Teachers				Involvement in the School and District				
Name	Grades	District Curriculum Committee	District Assessment Committee	Faculty Senate	Mentor Teacher	School Improvement	Articulation
Amonte	1		X	X			
Barker	5			X		X	
Benet	5	X					
Chan	3				X	X	
D'Mar	1						
Effen	2	X					
Franks	2	X				X	X
Gillan	3			X			
Horillo	k						
Janrette	1			X			
Jensen	k						
Kirby	4						
Lang	4						
Lema	k						
Moreno	3			X			
Nava	5						
Ogden	2						
Ono	2		X				
Phong	1		X	X			
Rameriz	3			X			X
Ramos	k						
Solario	4						X
Tupa	5				X		
Winaker	4	X		X	X		

Use a matrix to determine how involved a staff is at various levels and where they are investing their time. Also use the matrix to determine if the same teachers are assigned to multiple committees or task forces.

particular task, assessment teams, and committees for various purposes) are amounting to greater investments of time by staff and administration. When teachers complain about their time being consumed by meetings unrelated to student performance, principals need to listen carefully and collaboratively establish priorities for commitments of time and energy. Some schools have distinguished what is creditable professional development by looking at the impact on the learning of all students. If the impact is high, as in performance assessment teams, the time is counted as credit for professional development units on the salary schedule. Weekly meetings at grade levels to conduct business—establish schedules, distribute memos and give feedback, assign space, and so on—are not considered professional development. Meetings to analyze disaggregated student performance data or to examine multiple forms of student assessments certainly will affect teaching and learning and are indeed professional development.

A caution in working with the tool of encouraging people connections is that teachers are generally more comfortable with those they have worked with over time. They will routinely sit in the same seats with the same people for the same function, as in a faculty meeting, for example. Many new teachers have been reproached for sitting in a seat that is "reserved" for a veteran faculty member. In faculty seminars, staying with the same comfortable group while teachers are experiencing new strategies is sometimes a block to their learning because they may be reluctant to make mistakes in front of their close associates as they try something new. Experienced facilitators recognize the importance of varying the connections. Discussing ways of grouping faculty members is a good topic for your leadership team to grapple with, especially when they are planning to introduce new concepts to their colleagues.

Variety is the spice of a professional's life. According to brain researchers, adult learners crave novelty, creativity, and a variety of choices. As educators collaboratively design a professional development plan for their school or district, they must consider the needs of the adult learner. In providing opportunities for teachers to make new connections, they also address the systemic need of a healthy organization by infusing it with multiple perspectives.

Members of a learning community understand that they don't need the virus brought on by "public think" because they really can figure out the most effective pathways to graduating all students, given time, resources, technology, and district commitment, added to their passion for students and learning. Using professional development opportunities to think through the issues with their colleagues, they can learn more about the causes, examine student data, analyze the responses to standards assessments, and balance their learning with their experiences. They can look at students with fresh eyes as they figure out how to accomplish this enormous task the public has given them—to educate the youth of America.

THE TOOLS OF REFLECTION AND DIALOGUE

How do educators clarify their understandings and make meaning from education and experience? Schon's (1983) work suggests that a way to personal growth and development is through reflection. Mulling over what we have experienced is not what we are describing. Rather, reflection is a purposeful strategy for reshaping or adapting our behavior based on new understandings that result from gaining different perspectives of the problem. Repeated use of reflection as a habit of mind enables us to frame our future actions based on learning from our experience. Because modern life seems to become more frantic each day, reflection is not something we normally insert into our work schedule. In fact, it is a learned behavior that, for some participants, may have its beginnings in professional development seminars. When facilitators ask participants to reflect on what they have just learned, they are able to have more meaningful conversations with their colleagues because the initial sorting of ideas has already taken place. Schon's studies demonstrate that this self-reflection leads to continued growth over time.

As new forms of professional development emerge, including writing new curricula, collaboratively examining student work, analyzing data, prioritizing and implementing standards, constructing performance assessments, and coaching peers, the expectation is that because people teach in the same building or on the same campus they know how to be with each other. Do they really know the skills of inquiry, dialogue, and discussion, and under what circumstances they should be used? Learning to identify when advocacy is interfering with an open exchange or exploration of an idea is a very useful skill. Knowledgeable teachers, however, seldom remind their colleagues that there is a difference between advocacy and dialogue. Instead of investing their time with colleagues to learn the skills of communication, teachers have preferred to accomplish tasks in isolation. As they experience new collaborative forms of professional development, however, they will understand the realities of needing communication skills to work with colleagues to develop curriculum, apply new teaching strategies, and conduct action research. Dialogue, discussion, and reflection also give educators open space for thinking about teaching and learning. Becoming familiar with tools for implementation will help educators achieve both long-term and short-term results.

Few facilitators would accept the title of professional developer without having Bohm's (1996) text on conducting dialogues in their personal toolboxes. Sometimes faculties get into a learning situation where hidden or exposed feelings of hurt and frustration turn into explosive exchanges. The group may insist on putting everything out on the table. A free-for-all has no positive gain, only negative, perpetuated losses. The facilitator may want to open a dialogue after setting ground rules and demonstrating the differences in inquiry, discussion, dialogue, and advocacy. The purpose of the dialogue is not to get one's way but to learn of other realities. It is a safe place to test assumptions and question how one has previously thought about a given topic.

Bohm (1996) suggests that we don't need an extensive knowledge of personal history to have trust and openness in a group. We can use a dialogue where we give open space for others to talk while we listen and then ask thoughtful questions. It is aimed at deepening our understanding while exploring problems or issues. Participants come to the seminar knowing they will learn a new skill for use with colleagues or with students. Of particular value is dialogue around related concepts such as a reading about what students bring to the classroom in cognitive readiness. Another opportunity is learning about a person's experience in a new culture. Teachers are able to use their new understandings from dialogue to help new students. The dialogue can be extended as time and interest permit or conducted within a limited amount of time. Occasionally, an opportunity for ad hoc dialogue arises out of a need to solve a problem or discuss an issue. It is helpful when in a meeting the need for a break becomes obvious and the facilitator gets permission from the group to move into dialogue. The participants rearrange the chairs so that everyone can see the faces of everyone else in the room. The facilitator reviews the elements of a dialogue and moves from an escalating polarization of participants to a thoughtful exploration of the issues.

CONCLUSION

Educators who thoughtfully design long- and short-term learning experiences know that everyone involved should respect teachers and administrators' dwindling professional and discretionary time. Furthermore, the research is very clear that to have major impact on teaching and learning, practitioners must be involved in planning, implementing, analyzing, and reshaping the professional development program. The patterns that emerge in learning about design center on the purpose and the outcomes, how teachers and principals will be involved, where and when it will happen, how frequently, what levels of experience will be considered, and what the alternatives are. Careful planning using a systemic approach helps to ensure that programs reflect the use of interactive strategies, ensure a cohesive design, and align to the system of standards and assessment. Using POTENT as a planning guide helps to ensure high-quality professional development. As designers become familiar with the components of POTENT, they are compelled to ask critical questions in guiding their learning experiences. When the questions are answered to the leadership team's satisfaction, the program continues. When there are no satisfactory responses regarding a proposed professional development opportunity, the team may elect not to move in that direction. High-quality professional development designed to improve student achievement, fully supported and highly valued by schools and districts, is of vital importance to educators. Public school educators are running out of time to make significant improvements for the success of all students.

Stop and reflect on these key points and their meaning for student achievement in your school.

KEY POINTS

When educators invest in learning about which tools aid in the professional growth of their colleagues, they communicate the worth of the work.

- Using appropriate visual tools such as POTENT for implementing professional development opportunities can make a difference in how teachers perceive their work because it allows them to see both processes and results. Using a planning guide helps to ensure high-quality professional development.
- Understanding the increased reliance of all people on visual interpretations better prepares teacher leaders, principals, and other facilitators for using frames and organizers with large or small groups.
- To attend to an array of conditions that may hinder school improvement, effective leaders equip themselves with communication tools and explore multiple opportunities to connect with others to strengthen their community.
- Educators who are willing to examine themselves to discover how to be more effective with students and colleagues and who are willing to expand their capacities by trying new processes and approaches, are, in fact, building a learning community.

5

Evaluating Professional Development

SCENARIO

A standing committee for professional development planning met in the high school library conference room. Two members were new to the committee, two had served for two years, and the chairperson, Thien, was in his third year. Thien was eager to leave for his next meeting with the other coaches.

"In the agenda I sent, I asked you to think of professional development activities we have had in the past three years," Thien began. "What worked for you and your departments and what would you never want to do again?"

The four other members of the committee read through the seminar list and rated the seminars.

"The program everyone really appreciated was the last diversity series because it focused on how we were helping or hindering student learning," Marcus commented.

"Well, some teachers didn't like the first part, where they got into stories about exclusion," Manny observed.

"I thought that was the best!" exclaimed Isaac. "Before we looked at ourselves objectively, we couldn't understand what others were concerned about."

"Wait a minute," Thien broke in. "This meeting isn't about the diversity workshop. It's about getting our act together and presenting a professional development plan at tomorrow's faculty senate meeting."

Manny looked very pensive. "You know, Thien, we really need to look at an evaluation design so that we have some credibility with our colleagues. Right now,

I don't have any data to help us with this planning. I don't have a clue how people felt about our activities, how the program helped them with their teaching, or what impact it had on student learning."

Thien was thoughtful. "You're right, Manny, but evaluations are too expensive. We spent a lot of money on a design for our grant last year. I don't think we have the funds to do a big evaluation design."

At last Berta spoke up. "I have to agree with Manny. I'm not willing to face the other members of the math department with suggestions about this year until I have a proposal that includes an evaluation design." She looked at the others. "Does anyone here have an evaluation background?"

"No," said Thien. "Tell you what. I'm in a rush today, but I'll contact the district office and ask Marla from evaluation in the district office to sit in on our next meeting. Maybe she can help us figure this thing out."

The meeting was adjourned until the following Tuesday at 4:00 p.m.

ESSENTIAL QUESTION

How will schools and districts evaluate their professional development programs based on student achievement and continuous improvement?

Pause for a moment to reflect on this essential question.

IMPORTANCE OF EVALUATION OF PROFESSIONAL DEVELOPMENT

Historically, many professional developers have considered evaluation a costly, time-consuming process that diverts attention from important planning, implementation, and follow-up activities. Others believe they simply lack the skill and expertise to become involved in rigorous evaluations. As a consequence, they either neglect evaluation issues or leave them to "evaluation experts" who are called in after the professional development ends and asked to determine if what was done made any difference. The results of such a process are seldom very useful (Guskey, 1998a, p. 36).

School and district leaders who are committed to professional development need to demonstrate whether their professional development activities and processes have made any difference for their school or district. Generally, educators plan and implement but fail to evaluate whether what they are doing makes a difference for the individuals and the system involved in professional development. It is important for a school and its district to stop and analyze the progress they have made by evaluating the outcomes of their efforts. It is important to answer the question "How far have we come in relation to the goals and desired outcomes we have set to achieve with our professional development plan?" Asking this question allows the school and district to evaluate the achievements made possible by the professional development processes. Bull and Buechler (1996) summarize some key evaluation questions educators should be asking about professional development:

> All the rhetoric about professional development and school improvement, all the theories about program design and peer coaching, all the action research and collaboration in the world ultimately give way to a single question: Is professional development working? To be more specific: Is professional development reinvigorating teachers? Is it expanding their repertoire and improving their ability to teach? Is it leading to new roles and responsibilities for teachers within the school organization? Is it contributing to a richer, more positive school culture? *Most importantly, is professional development leading to improved student performance?* (p. 27, italics added)

In other words, is the outcome of the professional development initiative worth the human and fiscal resources that have been invested? Systematic evaluation of professional development that is purposeful and driven by results is needed if it is to be supported by the school board, administrators, teachers, parents, and the community. What has your district or school done to support effective evaluation of professional development?

Most districts and schools do not have a formalized, consistent process for evaluating professional development designs, programs, activities, or events (Guskey, 2000; Killion, 2002; Sparks, 2002). The common practice is to plan a professional development program and begin implementation without an agreed-on set of expectations of what "full" implementation and success look like. The rigor of evaluating such a program is almost nonexistent. The traditional questionnaire survey of participants after an in-service day as to whether or not they found the speaker interesting, visual aids helpful, and other parts of the activities interesting does not get to the heart of whether the professional development brought about change in teacher behavior and increased success for students (Loucks-Horsely, Hewson, Love, & Stiles, 1998).

Sparks and Hirsh (1997) emphasize the importance of the shift in evaluation from the point of view of teachers' needs to that of student learning:

> Ultimately, systemic change efforts must be judged by their contribution to student learning. It is no longer sufficient to determine the value of staff development efforts by assessing participants' perceived satisfaction with those efforts. While participants' satisfaction is a desirable goal, assessment efforts must also provide

information about changes in on-the-job behavior, organizational changes, and the improved learning of all students. (p. 41)

Multifaceted, long-term evaluation that examines professional development in some depth and tries to determine its effect on teachers and students is needed (Bull & Buechler, 1996). Evaluation designs need to be started in the early part of the professional development planning process and continue after the particular professional development activity is completed (Guskey, 1998a, 2000). Evaluation should provide information about the implementation process and should document effects, especially effects on student achievement. Evaluation reports not only provide information to teachers and administrators but also are an important tool to inform parents and the community on the progress being made in the school or district. When parents and school board members see the results of professional development, there is less skepticism about future release time or about noninstructional time being devoted to professional development activities.

The need for concrete evidence that professional development is making a difference is important for maintaining credibility with teachers, administrators, and the community. A formal evaluation process demonstrates that the school or district is interested not only in teacher growth but also in the growth of students. Professional development needs an ongoing evaluation process to ensure that goals are being achieved, that needs are being met, and that resources are being used wisely (Zepeda, 1999). Without systematic evaluation of efforts based on hard data, it is almost impossible to determine if the changes are sustainable and, more important, if the professional development activities improved teachers' abilities to increase student achievement.

COMPONENTS OF EFFECTIVE PROFESSIONAL DEVELOPMENT EVALUATION

Components of an evaluation process for professional development include the following questions.

Questions for Professional Development Evaluation

What are the desired outcomes?

What are the professional development activities for reaching the outcomes?

Who will be responsible for the evaluation?

How will the evaluation be conducted?

What types of data will be collected?

How and when will the data be analyzed?

Who is responsible for reporting and distributing the results?

How can this evaluation contribute to the continuous improvement process for teachers and increase student achievement?

Table 5.1 provides a systematic way of planning the evaluation process. The components and questions regarding professional development and its evaluation can be organized and clarified by using the guide. The guide is intended to help professional development planners, principals, and teachers focus on the desired outcomes first and then develop the activities that will meet those outcomes, rather than planning the activity and hoping for the outcome, which is usually the case. Evaluation planning helps focus on the outcomes rather than on the activities (Guskey, 2000; Killion, 2002).

What Are the Desired Outcomes and What Are the Professional Development Activities for Reaching the Outcomes?

Professional development plans typically have a wide range of goals, but they are often not articulated as outcomes. How would you describe your successes with professional development activities and plans? What changes have occurred? By whom? Generally, professional development results are reported as completed activities (e.g., conducted a series of workshops or a summer institute), rather than as accomplishments (e.g., teachers using inquiry-based strategies in their classrooms have higher student achievement rates in problem solving). Outcomes for professional development can be described as new abilities (knowledge, skills, strategies, attitudes) by a variety of individuals (teachers, students, administrators); organizations (departments, teams, schools, districts); and areas (teaching, leadership, change management). "Being clear about desired outcomes, articulating what they would look like if they were present, not only lays important groundwork for evaluation but also causes the program to be more focused and purposeful" (Loucks-Horsely et al., 1998, p. 221).

Who Will Be Responsible for the Evaluation?

Establishing who is responsible for the evaluation process helps in clearly defining the roles individuals play in making sure the evaluation process occurs. When various role participants take ownership of the evaluation process, they provide perspectives on the professional development opportunities, which in turn provide insights to the evaluator.

Table 5.1   Professional Development Evaluation Planning Guide

---

Directions: Use the questions and the planning chart to create a
Professional Development Evaluation Plan.

Questions for Professional Development Evaluation

1. What are the desired outcomes?

2. What are the professional development activities for reaching the
   outcomes?

3. Who will be responsible for the evaluation?

4. How will the evaluation be conducted?

5. What types of data will be collected?

6. How and when will the data be analyzed?

7. Who is responsible for reporting and distributing the results?

8. How can this evaluation contribute to the continuous improvement
   process for teachers and increase student achievement?

Desired Outcomes	Professional Activities	Responsible Individual(s)	Evaluation Methods	Data Required	Data Analysis Methods	Results Reporting	Continuous Improvement Outcomes

---

Teachers and administrators who share responsibilities for the evaluation process commit to a representative process focused on outcomes. When responsibility is shared, there is an understanding of how the evaluation outcomes were developed. Participants who are informed throughout the process understand when adjustments are needed to better serve both the participants and the outcomes they establish.

How Will the Evaluation Be Conducted and What Types of Data Will Be Collected?

The evaluation process needs to be accomplished in a variety of ways to provide information on the progress of the participants and to define whether the outcomes have been met. To help understand the impact of the professional development plan and activities, a wide range of evidence is needed. Evidence from participants in the form of surveys, interviews, observations, lesson analyses, performance tasks, student work, and focus groups can provide data that contribute to the evaluation process. The type of data collected will depend on the outcomes to be measured as a result of the professional development. Clearly stated outcomes for professional development help frame the short- and long-term data-collection process. If, for example, the outcome is to improve students' reading scores, it would be important to gather data substantiating teacher strategies that develop students' abilities to read (i.e., has the use of a teaching strategy increased student capacity in reading? How would we know? What evidence do we have?).

Evaluation baseline data on students (i.e., achievement scores, grades, attendance rates, discipline rates); teachers (i.e., assessment of current knowledge, teaching skills, and attitudes); and the school (i.e., related procedures, policies, roles, and the extent of teacher collaboration) are needed in the initial stages of planning to provide beginning data to compare with the results of the professional development work. Also, these initial data give a clearer picture of the status, abilities, and needs of the students, teachers, and school and should be reviewed as the plan is developed. Developing a plan without understanding student achievement and teacher and school levels of need does not address the specific professional growth requirements for expected outcomes. Understanding the abilities and needs of participants in professional development is critical and can easily be identified through the collection of baseline data. Failure to assess the current status and level of professional development of participants condemns the process to one-size-fits-all professional development. Further, it builds resentment among participants because their individual abilities and knowledge are not recognized and valued.

During the implementation process, participants should document their involvement, including types of training, follow-up coaching, and feedback. Leaders already have many sources to help with this in-depth evaluation, such as questionnaires, peer observations, school records and reports, student portfolios, student performance, and achievement tests.

How and When Will the Data Be Analyzed?

Choosing the means by which data are analyzed in the evaluation process continues to clarify the outcomes. Data must be subaggregated and reviewed for their significance. Do the data show evidence of the effect the professional development activity is having on the participants? The data analysis process is important. Involving participants in looking at results becomes part of the professional development plan because it reinforces ownership in the success of the process and anticipated outcomes. When individuals are engaged in analyzing the data, they inform their own practice and understanding (Lieberman & Miller, 1999; Sagor, 1992; Schmoker, 1996).

Who Is Responsible for Reporting and Distributing the Results?

Evaluation results often go unreported in the leaders' rush to the next professional development activity. Reporting and distributing the results of the professional development plan as it unfolds helps clarify whether the goals are being met, what outcomes are having success, and what the next steps should be. School site and district leaders, including administrators and teacher leaders, must be prepared to report and distribute results to a variety of audiences. This crucial step in the evaluation process of results reporting to key stakeholders should include the following elements:

- Goals for the program
- Activities implemented to meet the goals
- Individuals involved and their roles
- Resources used
- Participants' reactions
- Data to support the effect on participants, students, specific programs, and the school
- Recommendations for changes in the program

Evaluation results provide information on outcomes and on the gaps that need to be filled for progress to continue. Educators who are able to communicate the results of professional development contribute to an understanding of what was learned and how the learning was interpreted through the information-gathering process. Periodic reporting of results by a variety of leaders at the school and district levels keeps faculties, school boards, parents, and the community informed about the purpose and progress of professional development to improve student achievement.

How Can This Evaluation Contribute
to the Continuous Improvement Process
for Teachers and Increase Student Achievement?

The evaluation process provides informed results of the professional development initiative. It does not allow the typical responses of "We think it is working" or "We feel good about it." Evaluating the teachers' and students' progress and reporting it help inform the school's continuous improvement cycle. It clearly focuses the school and teachers on the needed next steps. Evaluation provides for informed decision making about which learning needs of teachers should be addressed in the professional development plan to improve student achievement.

The evaluation process must include feedback for teachers, the use of data to show evidence, and data about student progress or lack of it. Evaluation serves as a means to observe, reflect, and analyze the work. Administrators and teachers need to focus on the evaluation processes and results as soon as they begin to plan for professional development. Unfortunately, educators too often buy into reform initiatives because of the hype around the program. The first question should be "Is the objective to improve student achievement and how will that be demonstrated?"

The evaluation data—both formative and summative—help inform decision making. Common formative assessment tools include informal and formal classroom observations by colleagues and administrators, construction of teaching portfolios and student portfolios, and student achievement on standardized tests. The evaluation informs future work as each assessment event in itself provokes new learning and naturally results in enhanced teaching practice (Guskey, 1998b; Sparks, 1998).

Continuous improvement in schools must involve an ongoing cycle of inquiry that looks at data and the professional development program to determine if progress is being made. Inquiry into what is working or not working in the professional development program encourages a process of ongoing feedback. Adjustments can be made to meet the needs of the teachers as they learn new skills and practice them in the classroom. Through the evaluation process, teachers learn to examine their teaching, reflect on practice, try new practices, and evaluate their results based on student achievement. This ongoing reflection must be seen as a part of the professional development process and must be nurtured.

Effective evaluation programs should have both long-term and short-term objectives (Rutherford, 1989). Short-term objectives usually target changes in teacher behaviors, in the school, or in the curriculum, whereas long-term objectives focus on improvements in student achievement or behavior. Professional development can be justified only if its ultimate goal is to improve education for students. Monitoring results has proven to be a major factor for achieving success in schools and districts. Results-oriented professional development planning requires that the theory and research presented, modeled, and practiced in workshops or in-service settings be supported with on-the-job coaching to promote transfer to the workplace and to facilitate change in teacher behavior that will affect student achievement.

The professional development evaluation process has implications for principals as they provide leadership for their schools' continuous improvement. Principals must help create a sense of ownership and risk taking in teachers as professional development initiatives are designed and implemented. For example, teacher-driven action research involves teachers identifying teaching and learning issues of importance, trying out new methods, and determining their effect on student learning without fear of a negative evaluation of their efforts by the principal (Sagor, 1992). The results of their research often lead to a further cycle of inquiry, which deepens the teacher's knowledge and understanding. It is a self-renewing process that models taking action on new learnings and examining results. Monitoring continuous improvement of teachers' learning through effective evaluation procedures also reinforces results and accountability. We can no longer afford professional development activities that do not have measurable results. Although each person may be willing to be personally involved, the administrative and teacher leadership is responsible for schoolwide and districtwide accountability and results.

CONCLUSION

Professional development opportunities are designed for a wide variety of reasons, and it is the role of evaluation to determine whether and in what ways these activities were successful. Fulfilling that evaluation role, however, is rarely easy. It is important to get professional developers and participants to use evaluation processes to better understand results and challenges for continuous improvement. Being clear about desired outcomes for professional development and articulating them form an important foundation for focused and purposeful evaluation. Ultimately, the evaluation process must answer the question "Is the professional development plan improving student learning?"

Stop and reflect on these key points and their meaning for student achievement in your school.

KEY POINTS

- The role of evaluation is critical in determining the impact of professional development plans and the effect on student learning.
- Analyzing results throughout the professional development process provides indicators of learning and growth that should demonstrate increased student achievement.
- The evaluation process helps shape the development of future professional development needs based on student achievement data and correlated to teacher learning needs.

6

Rethinking Professional Learning

SCENARIO

Mariana: *I've been a successful teacher for five years, and now I want to become the best leader of professional learning I can possibly be.*

Darby: *How are you going to do that?*

Mariana: *Well, first I'm going to absorb everything I can about professional learning and how I can be most effective in working with other educators. The work is so vital! We're certain that students must achieve the standards of learning and performance, and I know professional learning for staff is the key.*

Darby: *Then what?*

Mariana: *Then I will find a model, someone who is the kind of educator I want to be, someone with high standards of personal efficacy, a commitment to professional learning, and an eye to the future of our profession. Maybe I can work for that person as I learn.*

Darby: *I think there's more to being a leader of professional learning than that!*

Mariana: *You're right! What do you suggest?*

Based on your learning and experience, how would you respond to Mariana's question?

ESSENTIAL QUESTION

What expertise, knowledge, and tools do we need to rethink professional learning in the schools?

Pause for a moment to reflect on this essential question.

Are you feeling frustrated because your school is not making progress? Maybe your students are not achieving, or, more realistically, some are achieving, but most are not. Are some faculty members apathetic or hostile and is support for change shaky? Is professional learning sporadic at best and nonexistent in some cases? You will know that you are a leader when these concerns keep you awake at night. Trouble is, we have heard many versions of these questions asked over the years, and they continue to be asked. Some of the most valiant leaders, however, rise to the challenge. In rethinking some of these examples, we formulated specific tools to help. The first tool is IMPACT: Investigation, Motivation, Planning, Action and Assessment, Continuous Learning, Technology (see Figure 6.1).

INVESTIGATION

What is the impact of your leadership in a school that needs to focus on improving student achievement? As an administrator, what do I need to know? One of the biggest failures of a new principal is lack of a thorough investigation when the principal is assigned to a school. Principals' investigations are important parts of their orientation. To gain an edge in a demanding position, principals must form big pictures of their schools. They may ask what norms and practices are currently embedded in the schools' daily operations. As an initial step, they also look at student achievement data to determine whether or not students are successful in this culture. What is the dropout rate? What is the persistence of academic problems, such as repeated difficulties in achieving the content standards in a certain grade? Are all students successfully achieving standards at grade levels? What are the rates of grade failure? Are certain students labeled "low achieving" and what efforts are being made to make certain they have multiple opportunities to achieve the standards? If changes are required to improve student achievement, what is the magnitude of the change? Successful leaders know how to access data to allow continuous monitoring of student success. In addition, principals should request that data be disaggregated by variables such as gender, age, or language

Figure 6.1   What Is the IMPACT of Your Leadership?

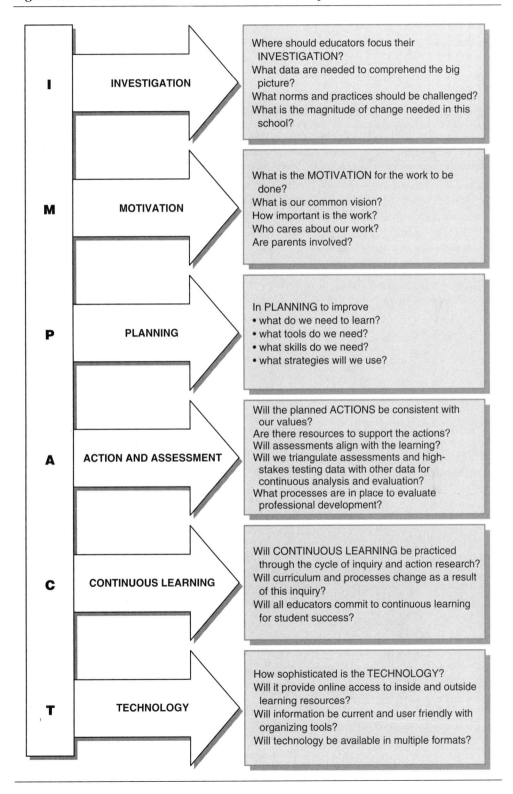

I — INVESTIGATION

Where should educators focus their INVESTIGATION?
What data are needed to comprehend the big picture?
What norms and practices should be challenged?
What is the magnitude of change needed in this school?

M — MOTIVATION

What is the MOTIVATION for the work to be done?
What is our common vision?
How important is the work?
Who cares about our work?
Are parents involved?

P — PLANNING

In PLANNING to improve
• what do we need to learn?
• what tools do we need?
• what skills do we need?
• what strategies will we use?

A — ACTION AND ASSESSMENT

Will the planned ACTIONS be consistent with our values?
Are there resources to support the actions?
Will assessments align with the learning?
Will we triangulate assessments and high-stakes testing data with other data for continuous analysis and evaluation?
What processes are in place to evaluate professional development?

C — CONTINUOUS LEARNING

Will CONTINUOUS LEARNING be practiced through the cycle of inquiry and action research?
Will curriculum and processes change as a result of this inquiry?
Will all educators commit to continuous learning for student success?

T — TECHNOLOGY

How sophisticated is the TECHNOLOGY?
Will it provide online access to inside and outside learning resources?
Will information be current and user friendly with organizing tools?
Will technology be available in multiple formats?

spoken in the home. Using data to monitor the performance of a school is a challenging assignment for school leaders.

MOTIVATION

A disciplined approach to motivation allows principals to do what others can't. A long-standing commitment to the concepts of motivation and discovery improves the performance of the entire school. At some point, motivation of staff may be an issue in rethinking practices to improve student success. The leader may need to revisit the common vision: What do we want for our students? What are the expectations? Are they high or low expectations? Do the expectations apply to all students? Do staff members agree that the work is important? Do parents care about student achievement? Do we foster deeper, more robust connections with parents so that we are working together for student success? Involving the school community is often motivating for teachers because they realize that parents want to be a part of their children's learning. When teachers give direction to parents, and the direction bears fruit in student performance, teachers are energized. Sometimes the principal just needs to ask, "If we don't do this work to ensure each student's success, who will?"

PLANNING

Leave it to educators to understand that planning is an important part of any endeavor. Frequently, as a plan develops, it leads to action—but not always. We recall planning with teachers and administrators to improve a school. The action plans had strategies, timelines, and outcomes, but nothing happened when the leadership changed. Key administrators and two influential teacher leaders transferred to other schools, and one left the district. Unfortunately, with their departure went the impetus to carry out the work. The lesson learned is that the plan should be so compelling, with such clarity of focus and so firmly based on the values of the school community, that it has a continuous power of its own. Planning for new knowledge, tools, skills, and strategies becomes increasingly important when the work is focused on student achievement. Although other needs emerge out of acting, a leadership team's anticipation of key elements accelerates the plan into implementation.

Chapter 4 includes POTENT, a compelling planning tool for ongoing professional development focused on student success. POTENT is an invaluable aid for administrators and teacher leaders as they develop a professional learning plan for their school. It is important to remember that the outcome is student achievement, and tools are only as important as the impetus they provide in leading the school toward the achievement goal.

ACTION AND ASSESSMENT

It seemed so obvious, yet one of the biggest mistakes in planning to take action is failure to align the action to be consistent with the values and goals agreed on by the school community. Researchers studying low-performing schools have theories about their lack of effectiveness. One underlying cause is that some educators may not intellectually support the premise that all students can learn. Trying to align a plan for all students to be successful when the values are at odds with the premise is a monumental hurdle. Until basic values and beliefs about students and their potential are explored and challenged, plan implementation is in danger.

Without lateral and vertical support for intended actions, the plan will flounder, yet as members of a school community create a school plan, they are so eager to act they may not explore some key concerns. Resources, for example, are often the last consideration. Leaders must ask, "Are the human, financial, and material resources in place to support these actions?" In particularly challenging times, state legislators and boards of education are compelled to understand that demands for student achievement and heightened expectations of teachers must have a resource component that supports the actions to improve the schools.

As the school community sets goals for success, assessment will be continuous (see Chapter 5). Teachers have voiced concern to us that their focus on high-stakes testing results has stifled their creativity. The authors believe that teachers must be more creative than ever before as they devise ways to motivate students to achieve. Teachers using standards as a baseline have appreciated having them as a reference for students and their parents. High-stakes testing is an opportunity for students to demonstrate their learning and for parents to monitor student progress in comparison with students of other schools. Standards are a unifying force for the curriculum in that they help teachers avoid fragmentation. An alignment of curriculum and assessment provides the impetus for teachers to embed the standards so that no student falls behind. Further, it is helpful to triangulate the data. Using student achievement of the standards, student performance on high-stakes tests, and student scores on teacher-made assessments provides a useful analysis of a student's total performance. In addition, triangulating data discourages teachers and parents from using a "snapshot" from one test to evaluate a student's success.

CONTINUOUS LEARNING

At the heart of a system dedicated to student success is continuous learning. The cycle of inquiry is a learning pathway complete with guideposts for a school faculty focused on student success (see Chapter 2). It is a process resulting in specific curricular and strategic changes so that all students can achieve the standards. To use the cycle of inquiry, teachers must be open to sharing their teaching strategies, content knowledge, and challenges regarding student learning. They need to share equally in analyzing needs as well as in planning approaches to improve student learning. Successful leaders and faculties are very comfortable with teams engaging in the cycle of learning, action research, and systems of evaluation to let everyone know how successful they have been.

When adults in the public schools have similar values connected to teaching and learning, they have a foundation for decision making to improve student achievement. The authors have listened to young teachers frustrated by some older, experienced teachers who stonewall the opportunity to change their curriculum to help more students succeed. In the eyes of beginning teachers, certain veterans appear to cling to strategies that no longer work for all students, and the context of student success is replaced by what is comfortable for adults. The adults in this setting have not accepted the concept of a continuous learning wherein each person in the school community accepts responsibilities as learner, teacher, leader, coach, and collaborator. Sometimes the roles are clearly and separately defined; at other times the roles are exhibited in a spontaneous, voluntary exchange of positions. In fact, experienced teachers could learn about how to connect with students from conversations with beginning teachers who are usually closer in age and experience to the students. There is no doubt that continuous learning is critical to the successful school (see Chapter 3).

In the future, as all people become more connected through values, networking, lifestyles, and economic and political necessity, isolation will become a conspicuous burden to a staff and will not be tolerated. Continuous learning will be the conduit for these professional connections. Margaret Wheatley (1994, p. 42) explains in scientific terms that, when we become synchronized within a small system, we have an impact. Synchronization can occur in public schools. When the goal of every student's improved achievement is clear, when commitment to the goal is universal, and when learning permeates the school community, the impact will be student success.

TECHNOLOGY

Technological savvy seemed like a long shot when principals were learning to use computers for communications and data delivery. But leaders who jumped ahead of the learning curve to bring technology to the classroom are already reaping the rewards. In the future, educators will increasingly turn to technology for professional information. In the past, educators made decisions based on little or no available data. Now they will be able to make informed decisions by accessing current information about each student. As extensions of their own professional learning, educators may also access online conversations with researchers, or they may ask researchers to identify practitioners in the area who claim expertise in using a particular strategy so that they have instant connections with information and help with processing it. At the same time, decision making may include distance learning and inter-networking to provide key information in support of improvement strategies, including data by cohorts, longitudinal information on results of using specific strategies, comparative data, and expansion of resources. With the student as a focus for decision making, teachers' demands for the tools of technology can greatly expand their ability to center their actions on student success. Resources are a necessary part of a professional's future as time for connections and research dwindles and demands for knowledge and expertise increase.

Armed with resources when they need them most, teachers are ready to face the challenges of the classroom. Resources should be available in the most user-friendly formats possible. As a standard procedure, districts should have current DVDs available, for example, on discipline, classroom management, strategies for teaching to the standards, curriculum content, or local history. These should be available to teachers at home or to teams at school. Lead teachers can provide access via live connections to their classrooms so that other teachers have opportunities to see master teachers working in specific content areas. Some classrooms are already accessible by cable at certain times of the day, so parents can see what their children are learning and doing. Researchers have not thoroughly explored what technology will mean for professional development. This support for professional learning as well as for data collection offers new opportunities for teachers that will only be expanded in the future. Technology is not the only challenge educators are facing, but to separate technology from students and their learning or from teachers and their professional development is to be blind to the outside world.

KNOW YOUR IMPACT

The newest dictionaries caution us that Americans are overusing the word *impact*. The traditional meaning of the word is "collision," so a discussion of a leader's impact on a school may indeed involve a "collision" of norms and traditional approaches to learning. The guides we describe are designed to heighten a leader's awareness of some critical components of academic leadership in challenging times. Included is a blank frame, an opportunity for readers to examine their own schools (see Figure 6.2). What is important for you to know in each of the areas? As the reader completes the organizing frames, other concerns will surface. The complex undertaking of changing a school cannot be placed entirely on a frame, but unless the described elements are considered in the change process, the leader and the school community will not be prepared to succeed.

Figure 6.2   What Is the IMPACT of Your Leadership?

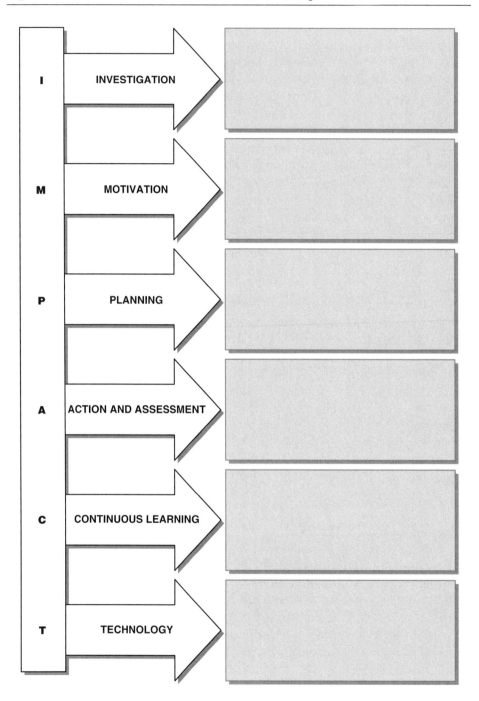

PROFESSIONAL DEVELOPMENT FOCUSED ON STUDENT SUCCESS

The relentless attacks on meaningless professional development are beginning to make an impression on school and district leaders. Integrated into the teaching and learning functions of the school, professional development will be the impetus for improved performance. We interviewed the principal of an elementary school after he had participated for three days in "Beyond Diversity" professional development seminars, studying strategies to help students improve their performance. He was in a very deep and troubled reflection about his practice.

"How will it be different for students when you focus on their learning as the most important concept in the school?" the facilitator asked. This mature principal thought about what he had done for many years, and replied:

> I used to think that moving students around when they had blown a relationship with a certain teacher was the wrong thing to do. Now I am thinking that the most important thing we do is help a student learn, and if he or she is having trouble with one instructor, then maybe we need to move the student into a different situation as soon as possible so that the student can focus on learning. I know this isn't a simple solution. But I also know that what I was doing may not have been fair to students or their instructors.

After three days of internalizing information and processing with colleagues, the principal was already into a deeper level of professional learning. He absorbed the new knowledge and reflected on his personal practice. He thought about a student's performance and hypothesized what did or did not work based on his examination of evidence. After sharing his insights with colleagues, he was ready to plan for his future actions concerning the teacher-student relationship. His justification was student success.

By necessity, more teachers and principals will rely primarily on their professional judgment to make decisions about how to help students improve their academic achievement. In the past, they may have deferred to a binding curriculum, thinking there was no opportunity for differentiation of learning. Mike Schmoker (Sparks, 2000) refers to such professional decision making as shaping the environment to get results. As professional development becomes learner centered, individuals will feel compelled to take actions that extend beyond a series of formal learning experiences.

JOB-EMBEDDED LEARNING

Now that the cycle of inquiry and learning has become a part of the literature of school improvement (our search of the ASCD Web site for "Cycle of Inquiry" resulted in 7,326 references) leaders may be lulled into thinking that job-embedded learning has no other models. We have included another model you can use to open the door to job-embedded learning and the value of this approach to teachers.

The first phase of the model is TACTILE (Training, Assessing, Collaborating, Trying, Incorporating, Learning, and Evaluation). TACTILE is a peer-coaching model based on new information and strategies and involves teachers forming partnerships to attend training. Experts coach the teacher partners and encourage them to put new concepts into practice in their own classrooms. The second phase of the model involves a similar process, though now a school staff is being informed and coached by partners who have achieved mastery. This model differs somewhat from trainer-of-trainer models in the past in that a critical part of the process is the training and coaching of school staff by partners (peers) who have achieved a mastery level of the concepts. The entire process will take more time to implement, but job-embedded learning is deeper learning because the concepts become part of the educational culture in the school.

This process encourages teachers to share their learning and encourages responsibility for implementation (see Figure 6.3).

WHY MUST PROFESSIONAL LEARNING CHANGE?

Just as parents are becoming more vocal about choices for their children by asking questions, making demands, and sometimes choosing alternatives to local schools, teachers will become more vocal about the kind of support they need to do their jobs in public schools. To be credentialed to teach in or administer the schools, educators take classes and schedule professional growth activities. By necessity, in the future they will seek an increasing variety of options to help them be more effective in their roles. Diversity of cultures, multiple languages, and varied social and intellectual backgrounds as well as learning styles all make demands on a teacher's effectiveness. Because students may have backgrounds unfamiliar to their teachers and students may have learning and language needs different from those the school has served in the past, educators are openly searching for connections and help. Professional learning can help to resolve teachers' demands for assistance and options when they need them most. In teaching, we call the acute need for learning "teaching to the moment" or "optimal learning time." Adults have optimal learning time also. Educators' demand for professional knowledge is justified when the results are increased achievement of students. Effective teachers need current content, the latest in carefully researched strategies, collaborative opportunities, and multiple pathways to hone their skills. In essence, educators have a right to demand the tools to do the work. Professional

Figure 6.3 TACTILE: Hands-On Learning for Teachers—A Trainer of Trainers Model

Teachers are funded for a training that includes coaching and follow-through. They form teaching partnerships as they invest in the training's concepts and processes by reading the research, practicing the processes, and preparing for implementation on a long-term basis. They understand and practice ongoing evaluation of the effectiveness for student learning. Following the training, they receive coaching and stay in touch with coaches throughout the implementation phase. Using their professional judgment, they determine if the training would be valuable for other teachers in the school.

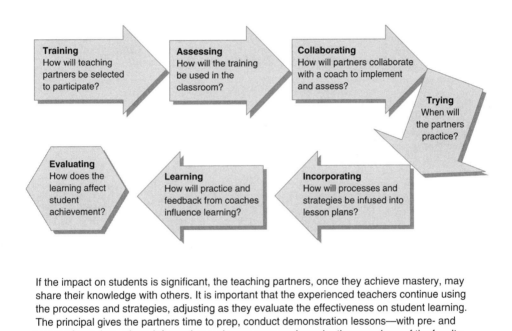

If the impact on students is significant, the teaching partners, once they achieve mastery, may share their knowledge with others. It is important that the experienced teachers continue using the processes and strategies, adjusting as they evaluate the effectiveness on student learning. The principal gives the partners time to prep, conduct demonstration lessons—with pre- and postconferencing—share information and processes, and coach other members of the faculty.

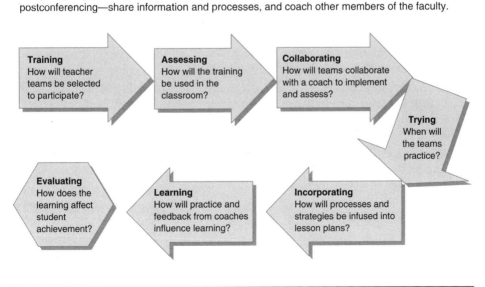

development must operate on the premise that every educator needs a rich, diverse portfolio of content and skills to be successful in the public schools.

- How will what's beyond the gates of a school affect a child's ability to learn and a teacher's ability to teach?
- How will teachers identify the help they need if their students' poverty, hunger, and personal safety issues are beyond their own knowledge and experiences?
- How will they learn what they need to know to teach their students?
- How will schools and districts assist teachers and principals to be more effective in classrooms and schools?

MULTIPLE PROVIDERS FOR TEACHER LEARNING

Districts, regional providers, state agencies, and universities will lose their influence as sole providers for teacher learning. New technologies enable teachers to reach out to connect with other teachers, in other states, in other nations. With international access to experts, teachers can search for their own professional growth support. Searching, even for the most adept user, however, can absorb huge amounts of time. The term *facilitator of learning* may take on an entirely new definition. A content expert facilitator could access specific sites and prepare summaries of what may be found there. The facilitator could prepare learning organizers with hyperlinks to move from one source to a related screen for different perspectives on the same issue. A facilitator could convene a subgroup of staff and make the arrangements to interact with researchers or other practitioners in a different city so that the teachers can take the new knowledge to their colleagues.

How many educators consciously limit their ability to know more about what they are teaching or how they are teaching it? The fascinating extension for the service agencies mentioned earlier is that segmented learning is possible, but it is not the way most people want to be informed about a topic. With technology, educators are able to cross subject boundaries as they access information about the economy, politics, geography, demographics, and culture from a single Web site. At the same time, they can look at curriculum, instruction, brain research, organizing systems, and content updates as they relate to the previous topics using other sources. With this knowledge available to all teachers, why would they even consider formal limitations on their learning to credits at a regional center or university?

- How will educators determine their personal growth needs?
- How will schools and universities meet the challenge of control issues, such as teacher and administrator credentialing, professional development units on the salary schedule, or teacher workday concerns?
- What agencies will support teacher networks?

SUCCESSFUL EDUCATORS' DEMANDS

Technology businesses may well be offering a glimpse of what employers can expect to see in the future workforce, for example, employees who are more loyal to themselves than to the organization. They demand greater respect and rewards for their talents, targeted benefits for their age group's needs, and opportunities to advance in their careers. Districts will have to rethink their traditional approaches that rely on financial incentives in connection with seniority in a district if they expect to attract and retain talented new and experienced educators. Some communities are already taking steps to provide housing for new teachers who are unable to afford to live in the area. Others offer incentives for teachers who become nationally certified or whose students all meet the standards. Still others have upgraded their professional development incentives and have institutionalized inviting teachers and principals to collaborate in structuring the opportunities. As districts invest more dollars in updating the skills and increasing the effectiveness of their employees, they will also explore new avenues for retaining their highly skilled and talented workforce.

- How will districts determine financial incentives and rewards for teachers and administrators who continue to demonstrate superior skills and talents?
- Will student achievement be a factor in the conversation about skills and rewards?
- Will access to excellent, diverse professional growth opportunities be an incentive?

URGENT NEED FOR COLLABORATION
FOR SENSE OF COMMUNITY

As self-help classes, support groups, car clubs, athletic clubs, day care parent groups, college and university alumni chapters, and virtual communities become a way of life, we are increasingly aware of each person's need for community. Schools are no different. Teachers' informal comments tell about the vitality of community within the school—from "I love where I work; it feels like family" to "I keep asking myself, do I belong yet? How long will it take for my ideas to be heard?"

Educators struggle with the concept of collaboration and community in our schools because they are not certain how to develop the relationships, create the common purpose, and foster a sense of attachment among people to something greater than themselves (Sergiovanni, 1994). They often try to create a common purpose superficially through strategic planning or visioning activities, but it takes an internal commitment on the part of everyone involved to form a truly collaborative, responsible, learning community in a school. Even neighborhood schools that seem to be natural places for projecting a sense of community often have teachers and administrators who commute, sometimes from long distances. Some faculty may resist forming a community with the entire neighborhood, yet it is becoming more obvious that educators need the school community. The more difficult the job, the more educators need others to stand by them and the more they need to stand by students and their parents.

One way to build community in a school is to start with professional development activities that focus on student work and then move to collaborative professional meetings about how to work with each child. Teachers who get to know their students and families, who can build trust with them and their colleagues, connect with parents, continually focus on what's good for students, and develop collaborative efforts within the community are beginning to invest in a greater concept of worth and respect for all.

Teachers need more recognition of their talents by the community. As needs for professionally competent knowledge workers increase, teachers involved in daily communications with large groups of people are obvious resources. If the community encourages contributions by teachers as knowledge workers, creative problem solvers, and multimedia experts in the construction of knowledge, then professional development delivery strategies must include opportunities to model and to practice all of these skills.

- How can schools build a sense of community that makes all adults and students feel a part of something greater than themselves?
- How can professional development build community?
- How should the community recognize and support the talents of teachers as professional knowledge workers?

THE CHALLENGE OF TIME

Researchers have a myriad of suggestions about how to connect, reflect, partner, nurture, network, lead, and grow in the profession. But as teachers look at the needs of their students, they are asking, "How and when do I concentrate on my teaching?"

Perhaps that is the greatest challenge for leaders. How do they help teachers concentrate on their teaching? How do leaders communicate a high value on teachers' time so that whatever else they are asked to do becomes less important if not related to teaching and learning? Resources such as teaching assistants, teacher aides, parent volunteers, and student teachers are intended to help a teacher, but there is no doubt that these innovations also take teacher time to coordinate, train, and monitor. Teacher collaboration is another commitment of time. The flipside of the collaboration coin, however, is doing everything alone, and that is fast becoming impossible. Somehow districts must find a way for teachers and administrators to reach higher levels of skills and competence through professional development while redefining their positions so that they and their students can be effective and successful (see Chapter 3).

- How do schools work collaboratively with teachers to structure their time to support the work?
- How can a school and district support teachers to reach higher levels of competence?

CONCLUSION

The future for educators is as bright as it has ever been. Leaders entering schools for the first time have a direction for improving student achievement as they step into their new roles. They learn that having an impact on their school means knowing more about how their schools are functioning, the priorities, the culture, the direction, and so forth. Teachers' earlier frustrations with the public's test score obsessions are being resolved. Schools are aligning their curricula with academic standards and in-depth evaluations so that students successfully meet the standards as well as demonstrate achievement on standardized tests. Technologically savvy teachers were exasperated with a need to look at data, without having the technology in place to manipulate it. Now schools are acquiring systems for compiling, disaggregating, and reporting data at multiple levels. A better use of technology for collegial sharing, collaboration, and problem solving is part of each educator's renewed commitment to student success. Multiple learning opportunities are becoming available whenever needed for teachers who will translate their learning into multiple learning opportunities available for students. Through a willingness to take on the challenges so that students can be successful, educators will make our public school system one that can respond with pride and accomplishment to public pressures for accountability.

Stop and reflect on these key points and their meaning for student achievement in your school.

KEY POINTS

- Leaders can use the frame of reference IMPACT for information about their schools. They learn to investigate, motivate, plan, act, and assess as they look at the systems for continuous learning and technology.
- Job-embedded learning has multiple payoffs when it is directed toward improving student achievement.
- TACTILE is a job-embedded process of training for trainers with multiple opportunities for teacher choices.
- Look for future opportunities for teacher learning through accessible technology, multiple dimensions, parent and public collaborations, and a community of learning.

Resource

Recommended Readings and Web Sites

Bredeson, P. (2003). *Design for learning: A new architecture for professional development in schools.* Thousand Oaks, CA: Corwin.

Darling-Hammond, L. (1997). *The right to learn: A blueprint for creating schools that work.* San Francisco: Jossey-Bass.

Diaz-Maggioli, G. (2004). *Teacher-centered professional development.* Alexandria, VA: Association for Supervision and Curriculum Development.

Elmore, R. (2000). *Building a new structure for school leadership.* Washington, DC: Albert Shanker Institute.

Elmore, R. (2002). *Bridging the gap between standards and achievement: The imperative for professional development in education.* Washington, DC: Albert Shanker Institute.

Guskey, T. R. (2000). *Evaluating professional development.* Thousand Oaks, CA: Corwin.

Killion, J. (2002). *Assessing impact: Evaluating staff development.* Oxford, OH: National Staff Development Council.

Lieberman, A., & Miller, L. (Eds.). (2001). *Teachers caught in the action: Professional development that matters.* New York: Teachers College Press.

Lindstrom, P., & Speck, M. (2004). *The principal as professional development leader.* Thousand Oaks, CA: Corwin.

National Staff Development Council. (2001). *Standards for staff development* (Rev. ed.). Oxford, OH: Author.

National Staff Development Council. (2002). *By your own design: A teacher's professional learning guide.* Retrieved September 30, 2004, from http://www.enc.org/pdguide

Sparks, D. (2002). *Designing powerful professional development for teachers and principals.* Retrieved September 30, 2004, from http://www.nsdc.org/library/leaders/sparksbook.cfm

Speck, M., & Knipe, C. (2001). *Why can't we get it right? Professional development in our schools.* Thousand Oaks, CA: Corwin.

York-Barr, J., Sommers, W. A., Ghere, G. S., & Montie, J. (2001). *Reflective practice to improve schools.* Thousand Oaks, CA: Corwin.

ON THE WEB

The professional educational associations, government agencies, and regional educational lab networks listed below can provide online resources and links to a variety of professional development current research and practices. These Web sites are included here to provide an ongoing updated resource for professional development ideas and planning.

Professional Educational Associations

American Association of School Administrators
http://www.aasa.org

American Educational Research Association
http://www.aera.net

Association for Supervision and Curriculum Development (ASCD)
http://www.ascd.org

National Association of Elementary School Principals
http://www.naesp.org

National Association of Secondary School Principals
http://www.nassp.org

National Middle School Association
http://www.nmsa.org

National School Boards Association
http://www.nsba.org

National Staff Development Council
http://www.nsdc.org

Government Agencies

National Center for Education Statistics (NCES)
http://nces.ed.gov/

United States Department of Education
http://www.ed.gov/
http://www.ed.gov/inits/teachers/development.html

Regional Educational Lab Networks

Appalachian Educational Laboratory (AEL)
Specializes in rural education
http://www.ael.org

The Education Alliance at Brown University
Specializes in language and cultural diversity
http://www.lab.brown.edu

Mid-Atlantic Laboratory for Student Success (LSS)
Specializes in urban education
http://www.temple.edu/departments/LSS

Mid-Continent Regional Educational Laboratory (McRel)
Specializes in curriculum, learning, and instruction
http://www.mcrel.org

North Central Regional Educational Laboratory (NCREL)
Specializes in technology
http://www.ncrel.org

Northwest Regional Educational Laboratory (NWREL)
Specializes in school change process
http://www.nwrel.org

Pacific Region Educational Laboratory (PREL)
Specializes in language and cultural diversity
http://www.prel.org

Regional Educational Lab Network
Links to ten U.S. regional educational labs
http://www.relnetwork.org

Southeastern Regional Vision for Education (SERVE)
Specializes in early childhood education
http://www.serve.org

Southwest Education Development Laboratory (SEDL)
Specializes in language and cultural diversity
http://www.sedl.org

Western Regional Educational Laboratory (WestEd)
Specializes in assessment and accountability
http://www.wested.org

NATIONAL REPORTS

National reports provide current perspectives on professional development. Frequently, professional developers search for documents to show to others who question the new approach to professional learning, and these Web sites are helpful resources. The documents listed are important current resources with a national perspective.

National Commission on Teaching and America's Future. (2003). *No dream denied: A pledge to America's children*. Washington, DC: Author.
Available at http://www.nctaf.org/article/?c=4&sc=16

North Central Regional Educational Laboratory. (n.d.). *Professional development: Learning from the best—A toolkit for schools and districts based on the National Awards Program for Model Professional Development*. Naperville, IL: Author.
Available at http://www.ncrel.org/pd/toolkit.htm

Sparks, D. (2000). *A national plan for improving professional development*. Oxford, OH: National Staff Development Council.
Available at http://www.nsdc.org/library/publications/results/res2-00spar.cfm

ADDITIONAL EDUCATIONAL INFORMATION SOURCES

Annenberg Institute for School Reform
http://www.annenberginstitute.org

California Beginning Teachers Support and Assessment (BTSA) Program
http://www.btsa.ca.gov

Coalition of Essential Schools
http://www.essentialschools.org

EdSource
http://www.edsource.org

Education Trust
http://www.edtrust.org

Education Week
http://www.edweek.com

Harvard Education Letter
http://www.edletter.org

New Teacher Center
http://www.newteachercenter.org

RAND Education
http://www.rand.org

References

Barth, R. (1990). *Improving schools from within*. San Francisco: Jossey-Bass.

Bohm, D. (1996). *On dialogue*. London: Routledge.

Bull, B., & Buechler B. (1996). *Learning together: Professional development for better schools*. Bloomington: Indiana Education Policy Center.

Burden, P. (1982, June). *Developmental supervision: Reducing teacher stress at different career stages*. Paper presented at the Association of Teacher Educators National Conference, Phoenix, AZ.

Burke, P. J., Christensen, J. C., & Fessler, R. (1984). *Teacher career stages: Implications for staff development* (Whole No. 214). Bloomington, IN: Phi Delta Kappan Educational Foundation.

California Commission on the Teaching Profession. (1997). *California standards for the teaching profession*. Sacramento: Author.

Christensen, J., Burke, P., Fessler, R., & Hagstrom, D. (1983). *Stages of teachers' careers: Implications for professional development*. Washington, DC: National Institute of Education. (ERIC Document Reproduction Service No. ED 227 054)

Cohen, D. K., & Hill, H. C. (1998). *Instructional policy and classroom performance: The mathematics reform in California*. Philadelphia: Consortium for Policy Research in Education.

Collins, D. (1998). *Achieving your vision of professional development*. Tallahassee, FL: Southeastern Regional Vision for Education.

Cooper, H., Nye, B., Charlton, K., Lindsay, J., & Greathouse, S. (1996). The effects of summer vacation on achievement test scores: A narrative and meta-analytic review. *Review of Educational Research, 66*, 227–268.

Corcoran, T. (1995). *Helping teachers teach well: Transforming professional development* (Research Brief No. 16-6/95). Philadelphia: Consortium for Policy Research in Education.

Darling-Hammond, L. (1997). *The right to learn: A blueprint for creating schools that work*. San Francisco: Jossey-Bass.

Darling-Hammond, L., Ancess, J., & Falk, B. (1995). *Authentic assessment in action: Case studies*. New York: Teachers College Press.

Darling-Hammond, L., & Ball, D. L. (1998). *Teaching for high standards: What policymakers need to know and be able to do*. New York: National Commission on Teaching and America's Future and Consortium for Policy Research in Education.

Darling-Hammond, L., & McLaughlin, M. W. (1995). Policies that support professional development in an era of reform. *Phi Delta Kappan, 76*, 507–604.

Elmore, R. (1996). *Staff development and instructional improvement: Community District 2, New York City.* New York: National Commission on Teaching and America's Future.

Feiman, S., & Floden, R. (1980). *What's all this talk about teacher development?* East Lansing, MI: Institute for Research on Teaching. (ERIC Document Reproduction Service No. ED 189 088)

Fullan, M. (1993). *Change forces: Probing the depths of educational change.* New York: Falmer.

Gardner, H. (1999). *Intelligence reframed: Multiple intelligences for the 21st century.* New York: Basic Books.

Guskey, T. (1998a). The age of our accountability. *Journal of Staff Development, 19*(4), 36–43.

Guskey, T. (1998b). Follow-up is key, but it's often forgotten. *Journal of Staff Development, 19*(2), 7–8.

Guskey, T. (1999). Apply time with wisdom. *Journal of Staff Development, 20*(2), 10–14.

Guskey, T. (2000). *Evaluating professional development.* Thousand Oaks, CA: Corwin.

Hargreaves, A., & Dawe, R. (1990). Paths of professional development: Contrived collegiality, collaborative culture, and the case of peer coaching. *Teaching and Teacher Education, 6*, 227–241.

Hassel, E. (1999). *Professional development: Learning from the best—A toolkit for schools and districts based on the national awards program for model professional development.* Oak Brook, IL: North Central Regional Educational Laboratory.

Haycock, K. (1999). Good teaching matters . . . a lot. In J. Richardson (Ed.), *Results* (Vol. 3, pp. 1, 6). Oxford, OH: National Staff Development Council.

Howard, Pierce J. (1994). *The owner's manual for the brain: Everyday applications from mind-research.* Austin, TX: Leornian Press.

Ingersoll, R. M., & Smith, T. M. (2003). The wrong solution to the teacher shortage. *Educational Leadership, 60*(8), 30–33.

Joyce, B., Murphy, C., Showers, B., & Murphy, J. (1989). School renewal as cultural change. *Educational Leadership, 47*(3), 70–78.

Joyce, B., & Showers, B. (1995). *Student achievement through staff development.* White Plains, NY: Longman.

Joyce, B., & Showers, B. (1996). The evolution of peer coaching. *Educational Leadership, 53*(6), 12–16.

Joyce, B., & Showers, B. (2002). *Student achievement through staff development* (3rd ed.). Alexandria, VA: Association for Supervision and Curriculum Development.

Katzenmeyer, M., & Moller, G. (1996). *Awakening the sleeping giant: Leadership development for teachers.* Thousand Oaks, CA: Corwin.

Killion, J. (2002). *Assessing impact: Evaluating staff development.* Oxford, OH: National Staff Development Council.

Kotulak, R. (1996). *Inside the brain: Revolutionary discoveries of how the mind works.* Kansas City, MO: Andrews and McMeel, Universal Press Syndicate Company.

Kruse, S. D. (1999). Collaborate. *Journal of Staff Development, 20*(3), 14–16.

Lambert, L. (1998). *Building leadership capacity in schools.* Alexandria, VA: Association for Supervision and Curriculum Development.

Lambert, L., Walker, D., Zimmerman, D., Cooper, J., Lambert, M. D., Gardner, M. E., et al. (1995). *The constructivist leader.* New York: Teachers College Press.

Lieberman, A. (1995). Practices that support teacher development: Transforming conceptions of professional learning. *Phi Delta Kappan, 76,* 591–596.

Lieberman, A., & Miller, L. (Eds.). (1991). New demand, new realities, new perspectives. In *Staff development for education in the 90s.* New York: Teachers College Press.

Lieberman, A., & Miller, L. (1999). *Teachers—Transforming their world and their work.* New York: Teachers College Press.

Lieberman, A., & Miller, L. (Eds.). (2001). *Teachers caught in the action: Professional development that matters.* New York: Teachers College Press.

Lipton, L., & Greenblatt, R. (1992). Supporting the learning organization: A model for congruent system-wide renewal. *Journal of Staff Development, 13*(3), 20–25.

Little, J. W. (1993a, June). *Excellence in professional development and professional community.* Paper presented at a planning meeting of the U.S. Department of Education Blue Ribbon Schools Program, Washington, DC.

Little, J. W. (1993b). Teacher professional development in a climate of educational reform. *Educational Evaluation and Policy Analysis, 15,* 129–151.

Loucks-Horsely, S., Harding, S. K., Arbuckle, M. A., Murray, L. B., Dubea, C., & Williams, M. K. (1987). *Continuing to learn: A guidebook for teacher development.* Andover, MA: Regional Laboratory for Educational Improvement of the Northeast and Islands.

Loucks-Horsely, S., Hewson, P., Love, N., & Stiles, K. (1998). *Designing professional development for teachers of science and mathematics.* Thousand Oaks, CA: Corwin.

Marsh, D., & Codding, J. (1999). *The new American high school.* Thousand Oaks, CA: Corwin.

McLaughlin, M. (1994). Strategic sites for teachers' professional development. In P. Gimmet & J. Neufeld (Eds.), *Teachers' development and the struggle for authenticity: Professional growth and restructuring in the context of change* (pp. 31–51). New York: Teachers College Press.

National Commission on Excellence in Education. (1983). *A nation at risk.* Washington, DC: U.S. Government Printing Office.

National Commission on Time and Learning. (1994). *Prisoners of time.* Washington, DC: U.S. Government Printing Office.

National Staff Development Council. (2001). *Standards for staff development* (Rev. ed.). Oxford, OH: Author.

Newman, K., Dornburg, B., Dubois, D., & Kranz, E. (1980). *Stress to teachers' mid-career transitions: A role for teacher education.* (ERIC Document Reproduction Service No. ED 196 868)

Ponticell, J. A., & Zepeda, S. (1996). Making sense of teaching and learning: A case study of mentor and beginning teacher problem solving. In D. McIntyre & D. Byrd (Eds.), *Preparing tomorrow's teachers: The field experience* (pp. 115–130). Thousand Oaks, CA: Corwin.

Purnell, S., & Hill, P. (1992). *In time for reform.* Santa Monica, CA: RAND.

Ramsey, P. (1997). The structure of paradox: Managing interdependent opposites. *The Systems Thinker, 8*(9), 5.

Rutherford, W. (1989). How to establish effective staff development programs. *Tips for principals* (pp. 1–3). Reston, VA: National Association of Secondary Principals.

Sagor, R. (1992). *How to conduct collaborative action research.* Alexandria, VA: Association for Supervision and Curriculum Development.

Saphier, J., & King, M. (1985). Good seeds grow in strong cultures. *Educational Leadership, 42*(8), 67–74.

Schlechty, P. (1997). *Inventing better schools.* San Francisco: Jossey-Bass.

Schmoker, M. (1996). *Results: The key to continuous school improvement.* Alexandria, VA: Association for Supervision and Curriculum Development.

Schon, D. (1983). *The reflective practitioner.* New York: Basic Books.

Senge, P. (1990). *The fifth discipline: The art and practice of the learning organization.* New York: Doubleday.

Sergiovanni, T. (1992). *Moral leadership: Getting to the heart of school improvement.* San Francisco: Jossey-Bass.

Sergiovanni, T. (1994). *Building community in schools.* San Francisco: Jossey-Bass.

Shanker, A. (1990). Staff development and the restructured school. In B. Joyce (Ed.), *Changing school culture through staff development* (pp. 91–103). Alexandria, VA: Association for Supervision and Curriculum Development.

Sparks, D. (1998). Making assessment part of teacher learning: Interview at issue with Bruce Joyce. *Journal of Staff Development, 19*(4), 33–35.

Sparks, D. (2000). Interview with Mike Schmoker: Results are the reason. *Journal of Staff Development, 21*(1), 51–53.

Sparks, D. (2002). *Designing powerful professional development for teachers and principals.* Oxford, OH: National Staff Development Council.

Sparks, D., & Hirsh, S. (1997). *A new vision for staff development.* Alexandria, VA: Association for Supervision and Curriculum Development.

Sparks, D., & Hirsh, S. (1999). *A national plan for improving professional development.* Oxford, OH: National Staff Development Council.

Sparks, G. M. (1986). The effectiveness of alternative training activities in changing teacher practices. *American Educational Research Journal, 23*, 217–225.

Speck, M. (1996). Best practice in professional development for sustained educational change. *ERS Spectrum—Journal of School Research and Information, 4*(2), 33–41.

Tracy, S., & Schuttenberg, E. (1990). Promoting teacher growth and school improvement through self-directed learning. *Journal of Staff Development, 11*(2), 52-57.

Wheatley, M. (1994). *Leadership and the new science.* San Francisco: Berrett-Koehler.

Wood, F. H., & Thompson, S. R. (1993). Assumptions about staff development based on research and best practices. *Journal of Staff Development, 14*(4), 52–56.

Zepeda, S. (1999). *Staff development: Practices that promote leadership in learning communities.* Larchmont, NY: Eye on Education.

Index

**CORWIN
PRESS**

The Corwin Press logo—a raven striding across an open book—represents the union of courage and learning. Corwin Press is committed to improving education for all learners by publishing books and other professional development resources for those serving the field of K–12 education. By providing practical, hands-on materials, Corwin Press continues to carry out the promise of its motto: **"Helping Educators Do Their Work Better."**